What If The Cross Changed Everything?

A New Look at John's Revelation of Jesus Christ

by Deb Moken

This Stick Publishing,

Mofire LLC, Sturgis, SD

Copyright © 2014

ISBN 978-0615987965

This Stick
PUBLISHING

All Scripture references are quoted from the King James Version unless otherwise noted in the text.

Scripture taken from the Williams New Testament, The New Testament in the Language of the People. Copyright © 1937, 1966, 1986, 1995 by Holman Bible Publishers. Used by permission,
www.sprawls.org/williams.

Scripture quotations taken from the New American Standard Bible®,
Copyright © 1960, 1962, 1963, 1968, 1971, 1972, 1973, 1975, 1977, 1995 by The Lockman Foundation. Used by permission

I don't know who to credit for the quote but I first heard it from Dr. James B. Richards. "It's not the person you believe in that influences you the most. It's the person who believes in you."

To my husband, Mike, who hasn't had a decent home-cooked meal in a year or two—I thank you.

To my dedicated Bible Students whose hunger for the Word gets them to class early Sunday mornings and late Wednesday nights—with a special gold-star attendance award going to Mark Shuck—I thank you.

To my friends who believed for me when I couldn't believe for myself—I thank you.

To those who graciously listened and encouraged the pursuit of this project—I thank you.

To my Brother—my Near-Kinsman Redeemer—Jesus, I am eternally grateful and it is to you this book is dedicated!

Table of Contents

Introduction

What you have in your hands is the result of a Sunday morning Bible class that lasted several years. We'd get together to explore the Word with an open mind and a determination to be as honest as possible with our previously held beliefs.

I never intended to become a scholar of the book of Revelation. In fact, I intended to avoid this scriptural labyrinth for the remainder of my days. I'd heard all the teachings, read all the commentaries, endured all the sermons that produced all the confusion and terror my little heart could hold.

No more, thank you.

So when I asked my class what they were interested in studying, and the consensus was Revelation, let's just say my reaction was less than enthusiastic.

Little did I know that the Scriptures we would explore had the potential to expel the fear, apathy, paralysis, and confusion, while leaving in their place exactly what was promised in Revelation 1:3—a blessing that leaves a person happy and empowered.

It has been an absolute blast diving into this book. All the controversy, mystery, speculation, misconception and craziness that often accompany the teachings from the ideas and images painted in this fantastic read have made the study an unparalleled challenge.

I encourage you to employ the same ground rules we adopted on the adventure:

- Use scripture to interpret scripture.
- Believe that The Cross of Christ changed everything.
- Hold loosely (if at all) any previously held beliefs or teachings concerning the book of Revelation.

To quote our Lord, "In seeing they do not see, and hearing they do not hear, nor do they understand" Matthew 13:13b.

My translation: When you think you already know all there is to know, have heard all there is to hear and have comprehended all there is to understand, you are in a world of hurt. If what you know about Revelation has left you feeling anything but happy and empowered please join us on our journey. You will not be disappointed. You will see how the Cross really has changed everything.

The Emperor has no clothes!

Hans Christian Anderson's endearing tale of how deception, illusion, vanity and pride is unable to remain in an atmosphere of honesty has long been a favorite. I have found myself in each of the story's characters: deceiver, deceived, silent doubter and unquestioning follower, at one time or another. But lately my heart has taken up the cry of the story's unlikely hero, "The Emperor has no clothes!"

This incessant cry rose from that place the Bible calls my 'inner man' and became the impetus for this journey into what has become the accepted interpretation of John's Revelation- the interpretation known as dispensationalism[1], an interpretation that became impossible for me to embrace after spending a quarter century trying to force my heart to believe it. The deeper I dug into the historical records of first century Christendom the less able I was to remain silent while I watched this "Emperor of Eschatology" being paraded up and down the streets of what is supposed to be Heaven's Kingdom.

I am not supposing to have cracked the apocalypse code and that every theory, hypothesis or suggestion I make between the covers of this book are iron-clad absolutes. But I do hope to open the door for dialog and investigation. And I hope others will become free to join me in a search for substance, plausibility, reality and ultimately the truth. That awareness will empower the Body of Christ to discard the interpretations that led and held them to the fear-filled, impotent existence that currently defines much of the Western Church. Instead we'll discover a place of faith, peace, mercy, joy, empowerment, gratitude, strength and love, which are the elements necessary for fulfilling our commission to advance God's Kingdom.

During the course of this project I—like the little boy in Mr. Anderson's story—have been told to keep quiet, implying I am unable to comprehend and embrace the currently-accepted interpretation because of ignorance and lack of sophistication. Even if that were true, the fact remains: The Emperor has no clothes, and I refuse to pretend otherwise.

I have also been encouraged to ignore it, told that if people are sincerely interested in developing a relationship with Jesus Christ, they will overlook the incongruence touted by the 'experts' in end-time teachings. REALLY??? REALLY??? There is an enormous credibility-elephant in the Christian world destroying people's ability to trust what is written in the Word of God. It breeds faith with uncertainty, crushes purpose and destiny, and we are supposed to be silent?

No, thank you. The only reason I would take that approach would be for fear and cowardice, two qualities frowned upon in God's Kingdom.

I do not relish the idea of being ridiculed for my refusal to swallow the teachings that so many are currently dishing up, but that is far better than denying the Truth of Christ's Cross.

I liken this to what has become of our nation's food industry. So many modifications, chemical alterations, processes and genetic manipulations have compromised the nutritional value of our food supply that disease and malnourishment are rampant. And empty calories are being consumed in unprecedented quantities.

To effect change in our physical bodies, we must honestly appraise our diet and exercise. The same principle holds true in our spiritual and emotional lives.

I hope this book helps people recognize that their spiritual and emotional growth may have been partly stymied by dispensational concepts hidden in food for the inner man.

Blessings to you, dear Reader. May you learn to listen to that ignorant, unsophisticated, honest little voice in your own heart that refuses to remain silent when lies are paraded for truth.

1

Purpose ~ Meaning ~ Relevance

The question concerning the *Book of Revelation* seems to be, "Why is this in the Bible?"

After we dug into the book, the most prevalent question became: "If it's not about us and our future, then why is it in the Bible?"[2] Which raised another question: "Why do we have the Bible at all?"

Why do we have the account of Egypt and the Promised Land, the Red Sea crossing, David & Goliath, David and Bathsheba or the Battle of Jericho? What difference does it make that I can read about the lives of Ruth, Sampson, Noah, Moses, Daniel, Elijah, Solomon, Elisha, Abraham, Sarah,

1

Isaac, Jacob, Esau, Joseph, Esther, Deborah, Joshua, Caleb, and Saul? Or, Mary, Joseph, Peter, Paul, James, Martha, Lazarus, Judas, Herod, Pontius Pilot, Priscilla, Timothy, and Lydia? And Jesus?

For what purpose have these accounts been immortalized in print? Because they carry deeper meaning than surface appearances, meanings that are relevant and applicable in my life today.

These stories provide opportunities to witness humanity being human. Sometimes, by inviting God and His ways into their situations, they got it right. Sometimes they excluded Him and got it very, very wrong. Reading these accounts of ordinary people facing life—sometimes difficult, sometimes mundane—the goal is to recognize yourself and your own tendencies.

The purpose of this book is to explore answers to three questions:

1. Why was the *Book of Revelation* written?
2. Is there deeper meaning beyond the surface appearance?

3. If so, does that meaning have a relevant place in my life today?

Why Was Revelation Written?

To find that answer, we must appreciate the political climate in which the book was penned—under first century Roman rule. What does that mean? Well, there are plenty of history books to give the particulars, but here are the bullet points:

Citizens of Rome had rights and enjoyed privilege.

Conquered people had only the rights and privileges Rome tolerated them to retain and maintain.

Caesar was deified and to be worshipped as god.

All people, including Christ followers and the Hebrew people, were forbidden to worship any other gods.

When things went poorly, Romans believed the gods were angered. That anger was thought to have stemmed from the fact that not everyone was giving proper honor, worship or sacrifice to whichever god was believed to be responsible for the way things were going.

Appeasing angry gods was a full-time job.

Christ Followers and the Jewish people—in their refusal to join the efforts to appease the angry gods—were
blamed for causing all the anger, tragedy and failure. Rome
could not be spoken of disparagingly. There was no freedom
of speech for conquered people.

Many Christians had left Judea and relocated in Asia
Minor (modern-day Turkey); the Apostle John (writer of the
Gospel of John and the epistles 1st, 2nd, and 3rd John) was
among them. He was the overseer of the church there. They
were his congregation. He, the Apostle of Love, loved these
people and taught them everything he'd learned during the
three and a half years he'd spent at the Master's feet. His
congregation knew his teachings, his illustrations, his stories,
his symbolic use of the Torah, his use of imagery. I've taught a
class for a decade, and my students know the meanings of my
illustrations, images, stories and use of biblical illustrations. It
is what naturally occurs when time is spent together.

John was present when Jesus proclaimed that Jerusalem was going to be overtaken,[3] its citizens enslaved, and the

Temple completely destroyed.[4]   John also knew the time for that destruction was fast approaching. [5]

John was also an ambassador for the Kingdom of Heaven, which meant there were tactics he was forbidden to use, including: fear, guilt, manipulation, force, deception and coercion. He couldn't even play the Just-because-I-said-so![6] card. What could he use? How about truth, love, honor, grace, kindness, mercy, and patience?

Here's the trouble with that. People tend to respond much more quickly to Kingdom-of- Darkness tactics. It seems we are wired that way. John had a big dilemma. He was certain of Christ's prophecy concerning Jerusalem and its Temple. He had a congregation to persuade that going to Jerusalem was not a good idea. Even of those who believed that Christ was the final sacrifice and were not trusting in the ritual of animal sacrifice, Jewish families had celebrated in Jerusalem at Passover, Pentecost and Tabernacles for 2,000 years. It was fun. It was a party. It was a chance to see old friends and have a good time. Think Super Bowl party on steroids. Human beings have always enjoyed a good celebration. Add God-mandated tradition, and it was a tough habit to break.

What could John do? The Lord's warning gave the time frame in which the destruction would take place, a generation:[7] within forty years, the old was going to be completely annihilated.[8]

The Book of Revelation was a warning to the Christ Followers (and anyone else willing to listen). Do not go to Jerusalem!!!!

This dates the writing of Revelation before 70AD, and more specifically between the years of Laodicea's reconstruction[9] and the beginning of the Great Jewish Revolt in May of 66AD.

The warning worked. According to Eusebius, Bishop of Caesarea, in his book The Ecclesiastical History of Eusebius Pamphilus, Bishop of Caesarea, in ten books:[10]

> *The whole body, however, of the church at Jerusalem, having been commanded by a divine revelation, given to men of approved piety there before the war, removed from the city, and dwelt at a certain town beyond the Jordan, called Pella. Here, those that believed in Christ, having removed from Jerusalem, as if the holy men had entirely abandoned the royal city itself, and the whole land of Judea; the divine justice for their crimes against*

Christ and his apostles, finally overtook them, to-
tally destroying the whole generation of these evil-
doers from the earth.

Anyone heeding the warning was, as promised in Revelation 22:7, blessed, happy and fortunate, for understanding and observing it.

As we will see, John used every legitimate weapon in his arsenal to persuade people to steer clear of the city of Jerusalem. The Revelation of Jesus Christ is that warning. Built on truth, it is designed to arm its readers with adequate information to persuade them to not return to Jerusalem. By showing how Christ satisfied the legal requirements making it possible for us to be free from the law of sin and death, John reveals what happened in the heavenly realm, the earthly realm, and the eternal realms both past and future. Are those things significant or relevant to our lives today? Absolutely! If the Cross changed everything, it's time to recognize those changes.

Why are there photographers at weddings? They capture glorious, life-changing events. When I look at my wedding album or see a picture of a wedding I was privileged to attend, reminders of the promise that filled that day immediately come to mind. The Revelation of Jesus Christ is the first-century equivalent of a twenty-first century photo album. It contains images of historical Heavenly ceremonies that changed the course of life on Earth.

This document reveals to us the events that took place in Heaven and on Earth when Jesus presented Himself before the Throne of God to redeem humanity. The Lord Jesus accomplished that by the laws of Heaven and Earth. His success changed everything: past, present and future!

Humanity needs to know what those changes are and stop living lives as if His Cross were nothing more than a parenthesis in the narrative of our history.

Yes, I'd say this book is most definitely relevant today.

Jesus once asked the question: "What is written in the law, and how do you read it?"[11] In other words, what perspective do you use in trying to gain an understanding of what is written? That same question needs to be asked in our efforts to understand what has been written in the Book of Revelation. The perspective used for arriving at the conclusions presented in this book has been—to the best of my ability—from first-century followers of Christ living under Roman law.

These Christ-followers' roots were in Jewish culture, and they believed, without a doubt, that the Cross changed everything: past, present and future.

With that in mind, let's see what answers we might come up with for the other questions on our list.

2

Someone Else's Mail

There are three things to consider before diving any deeper into this study: translation, speculation and interpretation.

The simple fact that we are living in the twenty-first century puts us at a disadvantage when trying to understand portions of the Bible. Unless we remain mindful of the culture, history, challenges, lifestyles, political environments, and values of the people about and to whom much of this book is written, the tendency will be to process what is read through the lens of a perspective that is two-thousand years and six-thousand miles off.

I am not insinuating that a return to a lifestyle that was lived 2,000 years ago is necessary to reap the benefits of God's Word. I am saying that some things will take on a richer meaning and clearer understanding when viewed in cultural context. Doing so does not diminish the power of The Word. God's timeless message remains just as relevant, but putting yourself in the shoes of the audience to whom these words of life were first written brings a sharper focus to the message. It is important to remember that when we read the Bible, we are essentially reading someone else's mail.

What Can a 21st Century Gentile Do?

RECOGNIZE CULTURAL DIFFERENCES

Remember that The Word of God, although written *for* you, was not written *to* you. Failure to do so forces speculation. Speculation is the process used when something does not make sense in the limits of a person's understanding, and it can result in inaccurate conclusions based on incomplete information, flawed assumption, and supposition.

Trying to make sense of ancient-Near Eastern communication with modern Western perspective breeds that speculation. Case in point—the Hebrew concept of the word *Front:* The past is seen as "in front" in ancient Hebrew thought because the past can be seen while the future is unseen and therefore behind.[12]

Or consider the concept of face/East/before: "The place of the rising sun. The Hebrews recognized the East as the top of the four compass points (contrary to our understanding of north) and the direction faced when orienting direction." It is easy to see that there are far greater problems that come from interpreting the Bible (regardless of translation) through the lens of a twenty-first century Western mindset than from the translation itself. [13]

Because the human mind is always working to make sense of what it believes to be true, it will take a bit of information that does not quite fit and, like a 2-year-old trying to put a puzzle together, will find a place in the library of the mind and cram it into that spot.

When I was very young the church we attended had a huge purple curtain that covered the front of the sanctuary; from ceiling to floor hung heavy, purple velvet. In front of that curtain was a table that held candles and offering trays. Every week—after the offering was received— the minister would take those golden trays, turn his back to the congregation and say to the purple curtain, "Lord, receive these offerings." Then he would put the trays back on the table, and I would spend the rest of the service watching the offering, hoping to catch a glimpse of God's hand coming out from behind the velvet to receive the offering we had given.

The body of knowledge my pre-school mind brought to that experience forced me to conclude that God lived behind the purple curtain. That is speculation.

The most effective way I have found to avoid this trap is by giving myself permission to create in my mind a category for things too important to force their fit —a category that says, "I must learn more about that." Then I put my mind at ease by asking the Spirit of God, Who is my Teacher,[14] to reveal to me if, when, how and where this important piece might fit into the puzzle of life.

Speculation leads to the kinds of conclusions that require complicated mental contortions to maintain them when reality challenges their validity: the earth is flat, the sun revolves around the earth, if God intended for man to fly He would have given him wings, women are inferior and should have no voice or vote. Speculation does not lead to solid conclusions.

APPRECIATE TRANSLATION CHALLENGES

In this context *translation* refers to recognizing the challenges presented by translation from ancient Hebrew to ancient Greek to fourth-century Latin to eighth, fourteenth, sixteenth, ... twenty-first century English. To take a document written in a language (Hebrew[15]) full of cultural concepts and ancient imagery and written by a people of shared history, religion, culture and political understanding—the probability of nuance being lost is undeniable.

Again, I am not saying the value of God's Word is diminished. I am saying that the wise reader is ever mindful of the fact that to disregard the obvious discrepancies between our perspective and that of people living in the first century under Roman rule puts us at a huge disadvantage.

When reading the Bible, remain mindful of cultural, historical, religious and political differences that may play a significant role in what, why and how something is being said. Natural human tendency is to adjust the meaning to conform to my sensibility, rather than to adjust my sensibility to conform to The Word of God. If the translators were not mindful of these factors, their translations would naturally reflect those same tendencies.

Jeff Benner, author of several books on Ancient Hebrew, points out both major and subtle differences that lead to very different interpretive conclusions.

> *"What may seem rational in our Western minds would be considered irrational to an easterner of an ancient Near East culture."*
> *"The authors of the Biblical text are writing from within their culture to those of the same culture. To fully understand the text one needs to understand the culture and thought processes of the Hebrew people."*[16]

One of the most important ideas necessary for cleaner interpretation is to realize the Hebrew mind which views all things as both fixed and active. Another concept explained by Mr. Benner.

> *"In Hebrew all things are in motion (dynamic) including verbs and nouns. A mountain top is not a static object but the "head lifting up out of the hill." A good example of action in what appears to be a static passage is the command to "have no other gods before me" (Exodus 20:3). In Hebrew thought this passage is saying 'not to bring another one of power in front of my face.'"*

Punctuation

A common misconception is that ancient Hebrew and Greek did not use punctuation. In reality, the function of punctuation is necessary in every language. Just because punctuation *marks* were not used in the original texts does not mean clarity of thought and meaning were absent. Punctuation was woven into the construction of the text itself. The original audience knew the rules of their own language, would have understood, and communicated the message accurately without the use of punctuation marks. Just because it is impossible to communicate written English without them does not mean Hebrew and Greek have the same limitation.

Sentence Structure

Without an understanding of sentence-structure-constructed punctuation, at times translators were forced to make their best guess. Sometimes punctuation placement was influenced by nothing more than the amount of space available. Add to this the segmenting effect that occurs with the chapter-and-verse numbering introduced in the 1500s, and the author's natural flow of thought can easily be lost.

Keep these factors in mind when something does not make sense in light of Who you know God to be, as revealed through Jesus Christ. Try adjusting the placement of a punctuation mark, and see if things come into clearer view.

Remember that childhood sit-in-a-circle game called *Telephone*? The leader would whisper a phrase into the ear of a neighbor. That person would repeat what was heard and so on, around the circle until it reached the beginning. It is a rare round that does not get things goofed up. What amazes me about the Bible is that in spite of the difficulties and challenges, the integrity of God's message to the world He loves has remained intact.

That message:

- God is God (I am not).
- He loves people.
- He had a plan to redeem fallen man and bring us back to Himself.
- He implemented that plan.
- Jesus fulfilled that plan.
- The Holy Spirit continues to empower us to walk in the plan.

- We are now free to choose whether to walk in that plan or remain under the delusion of our own making.

The Cross changed everything.

Life is found in Him, not a flawless interpretation of Scripture.

"And ye have not his word abiding in you: for whom he hath sent, him ye believe not. Search the scriptures; for in them ye think ye have eternal life: and they are they which testify of me. And ye will not come to me, that ye might have life"

John 5:38-40

THE FUNDAMENTALS OF BIBLICAL INTERPRETATION

Use Scripture to interpret Scripture. This is an absolute. A solid understanding can never be reached apart from this discipline.

Any attempt to interpret the Bible in any other way results in speculations. Many of those speculations have grown to unimaginable proportions, caused untold destruction and require constant 'tweaking' to keep them propped up. Furthermore, as appealing as it might sound and as convenient as it might be, the Bible must not be interpreted through today's headlines, current events or world history.

19

In 1799 a discovery made it possible to unlock secrets that had been hidden from the uninitiated for thousands of years. During a building-remodeling project, a rock with carvings was discovered. This terrific piece of history appeared to have no value apart from being a piece of a wall. However, this stone—discovered in a port city on the Mediterranean coast of Egypt—was anything but valueless. Because the message it contained had been carved in three languages, linguists were finally able to crack the code of ancient Egypt's hieroglyphics. Until the Rosetta Stone key was used to unlock the interpretation, anyone attempting to make sense of any Egyptian hieroglyphs missed by miles.

The same holds especially true with cryptic writings found in the Bible. The good news is that the key to unlocking the mysteries are not buried, hidden, lost or inaccessible. If you are holding your Bible (regardless of the translation), you are also holding its interpretative key.

In no book is this more important than the Revelation of Jesus Christ. Contained in the 404 verses of Revelation are over 500 references to the Old Testament[17].

Interpretation of Scripture is made by using Scripture itself. The story hinges on God's involvement in the nation of Israel and how His redemption was going to be brought into the earth through that nation. History, prophesy, symbolism, analogy and metaphor cannot be properly appreciated if not viewed from the Hebrew perspective.

LITERARY STYLES

The Bible contains a fascinating combination of literary styles.

Narratives

Narratives these are stories of people and events. These accounts were not written to persuade us to follow the examples. For example, Jacob had two wives and two mistresses. I can, too. No! Saul consulted a medium. No! David committed adultery and ensured his lover's husband's death. No! The Bible's inclusion of these stories must mean God approved the actions, choices and behavior. No, No, No! Narratives are meant to be interpreted in light of the commandments of God. Read in their entirety reveals the foolishness, danger and eternal consequences that result in ignoring God's instruction.

21

Statutory Laws

These laws reveal the righteousness of God and the standard that must be achieved (and maintained) for a human being to purchase salvation on their own merits.

Poetry

Hebrew poetry is interspersed throughout many of the Old Testament books. Hebrew poetry does not rhyme. The artistry is based on the structure of the text, playing on comparisons, contrasts, and parallel thoughts.

Prophecy

A large part of the Bible contains prophecy. In fact, almost every book of the Bible contains some prophecy. Like poetry, prophesies often use analogy, metaphor and hyperbole. Usually, a prophecy was of immediate relevance to the people to whom it was first given. One major exception to this are the Messianic prophesies concerning Jesus Christ. When prophecy is read, the question must be asked, "How would the original readers have understood this?" Placing prophecies in their context prevents the common mistake of looking for modern 'fulfillments' in prophecies, which were never intended.

Apocalyptic Prophecy

Apocalyptic Prophecy is a highly symbolic style of prophecy. The Revelation of Jesus is an example of this literary style.

Epistles

Epistles are letters written to a particular audience and often deal with specific problems. They teach us about dealing with our difficulties.

SUMMARY

Speculation is an unacceptable means of Bible study. Give yourself permission not to have everything figured out.

Translations contain some inconsistencies to the original text, but people of wisdom, willing to avail themselves of the instruction of God's Holy Spirit; can learn to recognize these things. These people recognize that the fundamental message of God's truth is stronger than a misplaced comma or translator's shortsighted prejudice.

BASIC PRINCIPLES FOR INTERPRETING THE BIBLE

1. Study every passage within its literary context involving the verses around it and its relationship to the entire book.
2. Recognize the social, historical, and cultural environment of a biblical passage, and view a passage in light of those differences.
3. Realize translations often reflect the translator's understanding, culture, era and paradigm. It is wise to compare several versions to determine the most likely meaning of a word or phrase.
4. Interpret any single passage in light of what the author has written elsewhere.
5. Interpret the Bible in light of the entire message of the Bible.

Armed with an awareness of this criteria let's wade into the deep end of the pool commonly referred to as *Revelation.*

3

More Than A Greeting

If you feel overwhelmed at the prospect of wading into the murky waters of The Revelation of Jesus Christ, know that you are not alone. With so little life-enhancing light having been shed on its verses, its message seems dark and sinister, rather than one of grace and peace.

If you have struggled to reconcile your understanding of the Lord, whom you love, with the grim picture so often painted by speculative interpretations of the images in Revelation, we invite you to join us.

It will be best for you to leave any previously held beliefs and ideas concerning end-time prophesy on the shore. Don't worry; they will be waiting, should you wish to pick them back up anytime you want if you decide that what you read in these pages is not more exciting and life-enhancing. This interpretation also fits more effortlessly with Who you know Him to be.

The Introduction:

"The Revelation of Jesus Christ, which God gave unto him, to shew unto his servants things which must shortly come to pass; and he sent and signified it by his angel unto his servant John: Who bare record of the word of God, and of the testimony of Jesus Christ, and of all things that he saw. Blessed is he that readeth, and they that hear the words of this prophecy, and keep those things, which are written therein: for the time is at hand"
Revelation 1:1-3

There is a high concentration of legal words and phrases in these three verses:

- Shew: give evidence or proof
- Sent: dispatched
- Signified: make known publically (for public record)
- Bear record: to be a witness, to bear witness, that is—to affirm that one has seen or heard or experienced something, corroborate another's testimony

- Testimony: what one testifies before a judge

AUTHOR'S TRANSLATION OF REVELATION 1:1-3

God the Father gave to [with, in, by] His Son, Jesus Christ, a revelation to show all would-be servants a quick synopsis of all that was accomplished through Jesus Christ.

This revelation is for those who agree with His Word and will corroborate their testimony with the testimony of Jesus Christ. To those individuals God assigns the task of proclaiming this message.

This document is to be used in showing any would-be servants (disciples) of Jesus a quick view of what transpired causing this new state of existence. He makes this public by or through His messenger[18], His sent servant, John, who bears witness with authority. He [John] confirms the word of God by corroborating that which concerns Jesus Christ and what he [John] saw.

Those who read, hear, understand and keep their eyes focused on what is written in this prophesy are happy (blessed and empowered)!

Points to ponder

Have you ever felt happy after having heard what most people have to say about this Revelation of Jesus Christ?

27

I'd have to say *happy* is never the adjective that comes to mind in describing what I felt after hearing the way others have interpreted the words of this book. Fear, terror, hopelessness and confusion—yes. Happiness, encouragement, peace, joy, edification—absolutely not. This is a problem.

Do I believe Jesus was the means by/in/through whom God reveals His Word? Yes.

Do I understand that the purpose of this prophesy is to provide me with a quick 'snapshot'—a brochure if you will—of the things Jesus accomplished to help me decide whether or not I want to choose to serve Him. Hmm—that might be part of the problem. Especially if I have always only considered this book as being a futuristic look into the final hours of human existence as we have known it. Perhaps my perspective is off.

Pondering Point #1: Can I consider changing the perspective by which I approach and read this book? If it is about what Jesus accomplished, rather than a picture of a catastrophic conclusion, then it pictures a beginning, rather than an ending.

Pondering Point #2: Is my life lined up and in agreement with the Word of God or are there areas where my life's story yet to come into full agreement with what God has to say about me?

Pondering Point #3: Will I consider making a diligent effort to bring my life and what I think about myself into agreement with what the Father says about me?

Pondering Point #4: Does my story align with Jesus' story? If I were called to the witness stand to testify concerning the things accomplished by my Lord, would my testimony be perfectly in step with His?

Pondering Point #5: Do I need a clearer understanding of what Jesus accomplished on that Cross know, as does John, how to speak on His behalf?

When these issues are settled in our hearts and lives, then—and only then—will the words of this prophesy cause the reader to feel happy and blessed.

4

Legal Documents

In Chapter One, we discussed some of the literary styles used in the Bible, but there is one style I wanted to introduce separately: legal documentation. The rules for legal documentation have not changed much over the centuries. They consist of these basic elements:

- Identify the Type of Document
- Declare Purpose
- Identify Originator
- Identify Recipient
- Indicate Date and Location
- Signature Certifying Accuracy

The Passage:

"John to the seven churches which are in Asia: Grace be unto you, and peace, from him which is, and which was, and which is to come; and from the seven Spirits which are before his throne"

Revelation 1:4

Remember that punctuation issue we talked about in Chapter One? Here is an example of that very thing. At the beginning of verse 4 the word *John* does not appear to serve any purpose. It is not grammatically connected to this sentence. Nor does it belong in the previous sentence[19]. It is as though John's name is simply dropped into the middle of this document for no apparent reason.

This would be very odd if what we are reading is a simple letter to the seven churches of Asia Minor. However, if what we are reading is a legal document requiring authorization or validation, and John is a first-century court reporter, then his signature is exactly where it needs to be if court reporters' responsibilities have remained fundamentally the same through the years.[20]

With that in mind let's take another look at those first three verses.

"The Revelation of Jesus Christ, which God gave unto him, to shew unto his servants things which must shortly come to pass; and he sent and signified it by his angel unto his servant John: Who bare record of the word of God, and of the testimony of Jesus Christ, and of all things that he saw. Blessed is he that readeth, and they that hear the words of this prophecy, and keep those things, which are written therein: for the time is at hand, John."

Revelation 1:1-3

The next five verses, with this punctuation change:

[4] ~~John~~ To the seven churches which are in Asia: Grace be unto you, and peace, from him which is, and which was, and which is to come; and from the seven Spirits which are before his throne; [5] And from Jesus Christ, who is the faithful witness, and the first begotten of the dead, and the prince of the kings of the earth. Unto him that loved us, and washed us from our sins in his own blood, [6] And hath made us kings and priests unto God and his Father; to him be glory and dominion forever and ever. Amen.

[7] Behold, he cometh with clouds; and every eye shall see him, and they also which pierced him: and all kindreds of the earth shall wail because of him. Even so, Amen.

[8] I am Alpha and Omega, the beginning and the ending, saith the Lord, which is, and which was, and which is to come, the Almighty.

Revelation 1:1-8

LET'S BREAK IT DOWN:

- Identify the Type of Document: *The Revelation of Jesus Christ*
- Declare Purpose: *to shew unto his servants things which must shortly come to pass and to bless for the time is at hand*
- Identify Originator: *God*
- Identify Recipient: *gave unto him [Jesus Christ]*
- Accuracy of the Transcript Certified: *John*

THE PARTIES INVOLVED ARE ESTABLISHED

This document is to be entrusted to the seven[21] churches which are in Asia.

- With the promise or purpose of: Imparting grace and peace
- It is to benefit: he that readeth, and they that hear the words of this prophecy, and keep those things, which are written therein: making them to be kings and priests unto God
- It is an indictment against:
  - o Those whose laws and ways are contrary to God's laws
  - o Those of the Nation of Israel whose laws are God's yet they killed/crucified the Lord

- It is coming from:
  - ○ Him which is, and which was, and which is to come; [testifiers of past, present and future events]
  - ○ And from the seven Spirits which are before his throne; ["seven" meaning complete and Holy Spirit of God]
  - ○ And from Jesus Christ, who is the faithful witness, and the first begotten of the dead, and the prince of the kings of the earth. Unto him that loved us, and washed us from our sins in his own blood, and hath made us kings and priests unto God and his Father; to him be glory and dominion forever and ever. Amen.

This is quite an impressive title: faithful witness, first begotten of the dead, prince of the kings of the earth.

WITNESSES QUALIFIED

John Establishes His Identity and Location

⁹I John, who also am your brother, and companion in [the] tribulation, and kingdom and patience of Jesus Christ, was in the isle that is called Patmos²², for the word of God, and for the testimony of Jesus Christ.

Revelation 1:9

The Tribulation

There are a few things to consider in this verse. Note the three classifications: tribulation, kingdom and patience. What might that indicate? In the Greek text the definite article "the" precedes the word tribulation indicating that the tribulation being referred to is defined and specific, as opposed to something general. Might this be telling us that 'the tribulation' was the state of human existence prior to the Lord's redemptive work on the Cross? Could there be a more apt title describing those centuries than when the one who ruled the world and humanity did so by fear, guilt, condemnation, accusation, death and hopelessness? Might the years between the fall of man in the garden and the redemption of man at the Cross have been referred to as the tribulation?

For the sake of this exercise, allow your mind to consider the possibility that 'the tribulation' may be a time in humanity's past, rather than a time in humanity's future. Might it not be the 4,000 years when man was separated from the life of God? When there was no spiritual life available to draw upon? When humanity was locked in an existence governed by a wicked, evil, ruthless, merciless and cruel dictator? A time when Satan wielded the power over mankind, a time when the law of sin and death reigned over every human being. That time prior to the redemption made available by Cross of the Lord Jesus Christ. Certainly an argument worthy of consideration.

Kingdom and Patience

It appears that John and his contemporaries shared three distinct realities: tribulation, kingdom and patience. Prior to the Cross was most certainly a time of tribulation. Kingdom is the time that Christ has made available. It is the state-of-being where God's laws govern. And I suggest patience is that place where the realities clash, and faith is tested.[23]

Patmos: Incarceration or Restoration?

The Island of Patmos was not used as a place of exile until the rule of Domitian, who reigned from 81-96AD. Long after the fall of Jerusalem in August of 70 AD, this Greek island on the Aegean Sea had been inhabited for centuries prior to it becoming a place of exile for political prisoners under Domitian's rule. It is not, as we might imagine, a desolate, inaccessible rock surrounded by crashing waves and treacherous snags as say Alcatraz or Chateau d'If. Today this

37

island is a beautiful, inhabited, tourist destination accessible by ferry boat.

It is widely assumed that John (who was the apostle/pastor of the church at Ephesus) was on the island of Patmos as an exiled prisoner, being punished for preaching the gospel message. That assumption is taken from this verse. For the sake of argument, let's assume this is not the case.

Doing the math tells us, were John on that island as an exiled prisoner, he would have been very, very old; not an impossibility, but certainly worthy of question. Could it be that he was there for a completely different purpose— for, perhaps, a time of solitude? Let's not forget that John was trained under Jesus Christ, who was of the habit of going off to solitary places to connect with His Father. Anyone who has served people as a minister of the gospel is well acquainted with the need to find a place of solitude for restoring the soul. John had been ministering and serving people for over 30 years at the time he wrote *The Revelation of Jesus Christ*. It is easy to imagine his need for a time of restoration.

A second consideration might be that John was in hiding. He was a treasure to the body of Christ. It is likely that, by this time, the majority, if not all, of the other disciples had already been killed. The body of Christ may have insisted he go away for his own safety. Antipas, of Pergamum had already been killed, so it stands to reason that other church leaders would be targeted, as well.

Another compelling argument is that fact that there was only one time in history that there were seven churches in Asia Minor.[24] Prior to the earthquake and its aftershocks between 60-62 AD, there had been nine churches in John's oversight. The cities and their churches at Colossae, Hierapolis and Laodicea were all destroyed. Laodicea was the only one of the three to rebuild. They did so with finances from the wealth of the Laodicean inhabitants during the reign of Emperor Nero. Roman historian Tacitus (14:27) simply notes: "One of the famous cities of Asia, Laodicea, was that same year overthrown by an earthquake, and, without any relief from us, recovered itself by its own resources."[25]

It is a plausible consideration that this document was written between the devastating earthquake of 60 AD and the fall of Jerusalem in August of 70 AD.[26]

"One of the oddest facts about the New Testament is what on any showing would appear to be the single most datable and climactic event of the period—the fall of Jerusalem in 70 AD, and with it the collapse of the institutional Judaism based on the temple—is never once mentioned as a past fact."[27]

One more thought before we continue. It is the word 'for'. This word in the Greek can be translated to mean *for the purpose of,* or *for the sake of.* Again, anyone who has served in ministry needs to step away from the pressing needs, cares, and responsibilities of that office for times of rejuvenation and reconnection. If Jesus had to, it's not hard to see that John did as well. When we look at the specific words given to the churches in John's jurisdiction we see that he was dealing with some very dicey situations. This helps to reinforce the notion that he might have actually been on that island at the invitation of the Spirit of God, find a place of rest.

5

A Coded Message

The Apostle John has one message: Jesus Christ has redeemed humanity. The significance of the sacrifice John witnessed on that Cross changed *everything*! John faced unimaginable challenges in proclaiming and establishing that message. With that in mind, let's consider the benefits of using a popular Hebrew literary style of that time: apocalyptic[28] literature.

Remember, this message needed to get to an audience who, at the time, was ruled by a foreign enemy—Rome. Is it possible for God to have chosen to communicate this game-changing message in a way that would be clearly understood by the intended audience, while keeping their enemies or casual observers clueless? Yes, by using the recorded imagery of their history, temple rituals, ancient prophesies and the Torah (the first five books of the Old Testament).

This particular genre[29], with which people were familiar, demanded the readers think in figurative terms to grasp the meaning hidden in the symbolic code. By choosing this literary style, the writer was able to effectively communicate a politically volatile message.[30]

Apocalyptic literature provided an ideal way to package and deliver the message and was used at other times when the Nation was ruled by their enemies. The prophets Isaiah, Jeremiah, Ezekiel, Joel, Zechariah and Daniel all employed this style of writing, during times of captivity.

Our challenge today is identical to what those first readers faced: to choose the appropriate key that unlocks the hidden message. This study is an exploration to discover which keys most easily accomplish that objective.

In the Spirit

Several Old Testament prophets provide insight to unlock the treasures held in Revelation. We'll start with Ezekiel.

Ezekiel was a Jewish priest, who had been taken into captivity during the Babylonian exile of the Jews (539BC — 598BC). His prophesies were specific to Jerusalem. They proclaimed judgment upon the city as the consequence of the depth of their sin. So when John describes his experience:

"I was in the Spirit on the Lord's Day,[31] **and heard behind me a great voice, as of a trumpet,"**

Revelation 1:10

This would have sounded to the Hebrew ear much like:

"Then the spirit took me up, and I heard behind me a voice of a great rushing..."

Ezekiel 3:12a

The people John was writing to would have recognized this immediately and made a correlation between Ezekiel's prophetic messages proclaiming the destruction of Jerusalem and the First Temple under the reign of King Nebuchadnezzar (some 600 years prior), and what they were about to read.

Also, Ezekiel recorded many accounts of his having been granted temporary access to view into the realm of the

Spirit beyond the confines of time and space. This appears to be the same type of experience John had and was commissioned to record.

The Lord's Day

"The day of the Lord" or "the Lord's day" is a phrase used 26 times in the Old Testament, and all instances are found in the prophetic literature. It is used in reference to judgment, warning, a description of past judgment, an admonition against false prophets, the destruction of Jerusalem, and in one instance might possibly be referring to the final judgment of the world. The phrase must be read in context to determine upon whom a judgment is directed.

Heard Behind Me a Great Voice as of a Trumpet

Notice that both Ezekiel and John heard a voice behind them. However, the New Covenant recorder turns, looks behind to see, whereas the Old Covenant recorder did not. Does this mean a turn chronologically, perceptively, or doctrinally?

Chronologically John may be seeing, in the spirit realm, what had happened previously. Whereas Ezekiel was a witness to what was currently taking place and what was going to transpire in the future. A perception change would make sense as well. What humans are capable of comprehending in the realm of finite time and space changes radically when those limits are removed. The natural result of this kind of experience would be a change in doctrinal belief. I am convinced John turned in every way necessary.

Another marked difference is the sound they heard. Ezekiel heard a sound of rushing (quaking, rattling, shaking), whereas John heard a trumpet.

Since one of the celebration feasts God had ordained is called the Feast of Trumpets, The Memorial of Triumph, and The Shout of Joy, let's see if the mention of a trumpet sounding might give a healthy clue to follow.

A QUICK SUMMERY OF THE HEBREW FEASTS: SPRING AND FALL, WITH ONE IN BETWEEN:

Spring Feasts

Spring Feasts are observed every year in the Jewish month of Nissan[32]. They include:

- Passover. A celebration to commemorate the Israelites delivery from the bondage of Egypt, and how death passed over the households that marked their doors with the blood of the sacrificial lamb.
- Unleavened Bread. This feast begins the day after Passover. Its observance serves to remind the people that when the time of their deliverance came, there was no time to wait for the day's bread to rise. Jesus also used leaven to teach how sin and false teaching affects every area of life.
- First Fruits. A week plus a day (eight days in all) set apart to celebrate and commemorate God's communion with man.

We easily see how these rituals symbolically represented the Lord and His ministry to humanity.

Pentecost

The feast in between spring and fall is Pentecost. It takes place 50 days from the beginning of Passover and commemorates the time when God gave the Torah (instruction) to Moses on Mt. Sinai. In Acts Chapter 2, we read how

God gave His Spirit to mankind during the celebration of the first Pentecost after the Lord's Resurrection.

Fall Feasts

The Fall Feasts are all celebrated the seventh month of the Hebrew calendar year, Tishri[33]. They are:

Feast of Trumpets[34]

The Feast of Trumpets[35] is celebrated on the first day of that seventh month. This day is unlike any other Sabbath. No one is to labor, offerings were made, and it is to be commemorated by blowing a trumpet. Eight days after the Feast of Trumpets is the most solemn and holy of Hebrew days: Yom Kippur, The Day of Atonement[36]. The ten days, which begin on the Feast of Trumpets and end on Yom Kippur, are known as the Ten Days of Repentance. This is followed, four days later, on the 15th, by the seven-day celebration called The Feast of Tabernacles. The next day is The Eighth Day Assembly, followed by the Celebrating of the Torah and final day of the Fall Feasts.

Today, it is commonly taught that Christ fulfilled the spring festivals with His Life, Death and Resurrection. The Holy Spirit took care of Pentecost, but it is taught that the fall festivals are not going to see their fulfillment until some future date, presumably when Jesus returns. I don't mean to be so contrary, but what part of, "it is finished," means "except for all the things that are not finished?"

When the Lord, following His Resurrection, declared:

"... All power is given unto me in heaven and in earth."

Matthew 28:18

I choose to believe that He meant there were no last-minute surprises, no legal loopholes or satanic shenanigans left for Him to deal with. He did **not** say, "All power is given me, except for the power Satan has not yet surrendered, and in a couple thousand years I will be ready to track him down and wrestle from him."

Perhaps it's worth our consideration that the trumpet blast John heard marked the beginning of the fall feasts, as they too are about to be fulfilled by the Lord Jesus Christ.

What did the voice say?

I Started It and This Is How I Finished It

[11]Saying, I am Alpha and Omega, the first and the last: and, What thou seest, write in a book, and send it unto the seven churches which are in Asia; unto Ephesus, and unto Smyrna, and unto Pergomos, and unto Thyatira, and unto Sardis, and unto Philadelphia, and unto Laodicea. [12]And I turned to see the voice that spake with me. And being turned, I saw seven golden candlesticks"

Revelation 1:11-12

Why is the Lord introducing Himself to John? This is a man who had known Him on the earth, believed Jesus to be the Son of God, Redeemer of man, the One Who was with God from the very beginning (we can read that in his other writings, see John 1:1-14). And remember, John was the only one of Jesus' disciples, who actually witnessed the Lord's crucifixion and heard Him cry out on the Cross, "It is finished!"

John is told to write what he sees and send the record to the seven churches of Asia Minor[37] (located in what is now Turkey). This was the region where John lived, and as an Apostle, would certainly have been an able and honored overseer of these churches while pastoring the church of Ephesus.

49

The First and the Last What?

Traditionally, the tendency has been to associate this with humanity's conception and conclusion. I disagree. Because this document describes the legal proceedings that surround mankind's redemption and the fact that this could only be accomplished by God through the higher laws of mercy[38] and covenant relationship—I am convinced that Jesus, The Alpha and Omega, Beginning and End is referencing the covenant. He initiated that covenant; He fulfilled that covenant.

Again, this may require an adjustment in previously held ideas, but I encourage you to make the effort. This one tiny adjustment will determine whether your journey through this book will find you ending up in a place of peace and empowerment or crouching in a corner hiding from an unknown enemy and anticipating an uncertain future.

And Being Turned OR
Once I Got My Thinking Corrected I Was Able to See

Verse 12: "And I turned to see the voice and being turned I saw..." This verse is worth slowing down to take a look at as well. The word turned means: to turn to; to the worship of the true God; to cause to return; to bring back:

    a. To the love and obedience of God

    b. To the love for the children

    c. To love wisdom and righteousness

"And being turned I saw..." This sounds as if John needed to have a change of perspective, attitude and heart, and when he'd succeeded at that, things became clear. This verse could have been translated:

I had to repent to comprehend what was said. After I repented I was able to see what I hadn't seen before: seven golden candlesticks...

What if the Cross Changed Everything?

6

The Ultimate Sacrifice

¹³ And in the midst of the seven candlesticks one like unto the Son of man, clothed with a garment down to the foot, and girt about the paps with a golden girdle. ¹⁴ His head and his hairs were white like wool, as white as snow; and his eyes were as a flame of fire; ¹⁵ And his feet like unto fine brass, as if they burned in a furnace; and his voice as the sound of many waters.

Revelation 1:13-15

In this chapter we're going to examine the order and ritual of Hebrew worship in the Temple/Tabernacle.

The Tabernacle

The Tabernacle[39] was divided into three sections:

    A. The outer court

    B. The Holy Place

    C. The Most Holy Place (Holy of Holies)

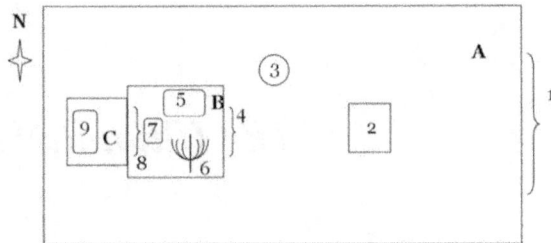

    1. The Gate The only access point into the tabernacle was this 20-cubit[40]-wide gate.

    2. The Brazen (bronze) Altar for burnt sacrifice

    3. The Bronze Water Basin

    4. The Door

    5. The Gold Table of Showbread

    6. The Gold Seven-Stemmed Candle Stand (Lamp)

    7. Gold Altar of Incense

    8. The Veil

    9. The Ark of the Covenant & The Mercy Seat

    Every Hebrew person, who had ever participated in Temple Worship, was well acquainted with this image. It is etched in their minds, although the meaning is often lost or overlooked in ours. The symbolism is simple to understand when we remember the goal: to be in the presence of the Father enjoying a relationship with Him that is one-on-one and face-to-face.

Translation of the Tabernacle Worship Model

There is only one starting, beginning place (the Gate). Anyone who desires a relationship with the Father must understand that there is only one entrance into that Holy conversation: the gate.[41] It is wide and accommodating. All are invited to the outer court. It is a place that represents the physical aspect of our beings. An acceptable offering and sacrifice was brought into this place where priests were charged with the responsibility to present those gifts to God in a way that meticulously followed His instructions[42].

This was a daily ritual, but on that most Holy of Holi(y)days,—The Day of the Lord—the High Priest was the only one to perform the ritual. On this Holy day, he alone fulfilled the necessary tasks that culminated with his entering into the Holy of Holies—the place where God's presence dwelt—to present the once-a-year offering of the blood from the bull that had been sacrificed for the sins of the entire nation.

This was the closest any human being was able to get to the presence of God on the earth.

Gold or Brass?

Gold represents heaven. Brass (bronze)—although it might look like gold, is not—speaks of the earthly appearance of heavenly things. Brass also relates to judgment and earthly substitutional sacrifice. In John's description of the Lord's feet, he is saying that these feet walked on the earth, and this man was humanity's sacrifice.

John is telling his readers that he saw Jesus, on the Day of Atonement, as both the sacrifice and the High Priest.[43] How do we know that? Here are the clues: He was clothed in a garment down to His feet. His chest was covered in gold, his head and hair described the way Moses looked after having been in the presence of God.[44]

SYMBOLIC OR LITERAL INTERPRETATION?

[16] "And he had in his right hand seven stars: and out of his mouth went a sharp two-edged sword: and his countenance was as the sun shineth in his strength"

Revelation 1:16

Here is a rather disturbing image—if taken literally—a sword protruding from a man's mouth. What might that mean?

"...sword of the spirit, which is the Word of God"

Ephesians 6:17

"For the word of God is living and powerful, and sharper than any two-edged sword, piercing even to the division of soul and spirit, and of joints and marrow, and is a discerner of the thoughts and intents of the heart"

Hebrews 4:12

The sharp, two-edged sword used by the Lord to divide (separate/judge) the thoughts and intent of the human heart is not a weapon of forged steel. It is Words of Truth.

[17] "And when I saw him, I fell at his feet as dead. And he laid his right hand upon me, saying unto me, Fear not; I am the first and the last:

[18]I am he that liveth, and was dead; and, behold, I am alive for evermore, Amen; and have the keys of hell and of death"

Revelation 1:17-18

Those are the words of truth! The testimony Christ Jesus is presenting in the Court of Heaven, and we, who are presently confined to the earth, can take and transform our lives if these words are judged to be true.

Keys

This is a perfect time to illustrate how to use the Bible to interpret the Bible. We read in Matthew 16:15-21 where the Lord asked His disciples who they thought He was, and Peter said, "Thou are the Christ, the Son of the Living God." Jesus goes on to say that Peter had received that revelation straight from God, the Father. In verse 18 we learn that it is the foundation of *that* revelation—*Jesus is the Christ, Son of the Living God*—upon which the church will be built; and that this truth is the key to unlock and release the power of God's Kingdom.

The Key: Jesus is the Christ—Son of the Living God! This truth cannot be fully understood from an earthly, flesh-

and-blood perspective. It is a spiritual truth revealed to the hearts of people by the Spirit of God, the Father, to anyone thirsty to find it.

[19] **"Write the things which thou hast seen, and the things which are, and the things which shall be hereafter"**

Revelation 1:19

Consider the verb tenses used:

- Hast seen—past tense—the way things were
- Which are—present tense—the way things are
- Which shall be—future tense—the way things will be

It's important to remember that what John is about to witness includes historical, current and future events.

INTERPRETIVE TRANSLATION KEYS

[20]**The mystery of the seven stars which thou sawest in my right hand, and the seven golden candlesticks. The seven stars are the angels of the seven churches: and the seven candlesticks which thou sawest are the seven churches"**

Revelation 1:20

Here we are made to clearly understand that the images John saw are to be understood symbolically not literally:

- Star—the one responsible to deliver the message
- Candlestick—the ones responsible to receive the message and give it a platform upon which to reside—the church

TEMPLE IMAGERY—JESUS IS THE WAY

*"Jesus saith unto him, I am **the way**, **the** truth, and **the** life: no man cometh unto **the** Father, but by me"*

(emphasis added) John 14:6

The purpose of the candlestick in Temple worship was to provide light for The Holy Place, as it also lights the path that leads to The Most Holy Place—the presence of the Father.

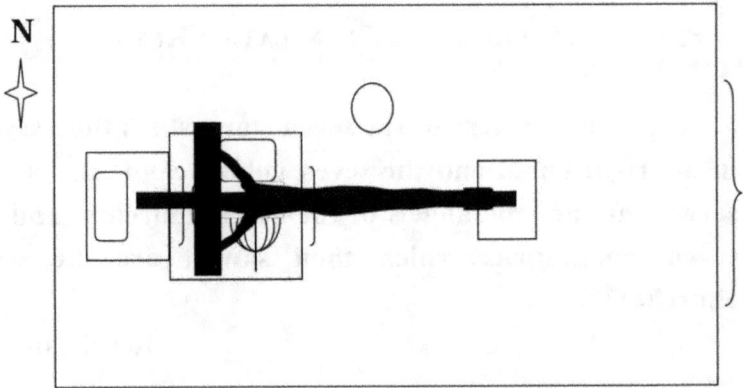

The use of this imagery communicates clearly Heaven's intention for the church: be a carrier of Light and Truth to a world lost in darkness. The appointed leaders and the congregations are entrusted with the truth that lights humanity's way to the presence of the Father.

Jesus is the Way because he alone made the way. He is the Gate. He is the Sacrifice. He is the Door. He is the Veil. He is the High Priest. He is the Blood. He is the Atonement. He is the Redeemer. He is the Mediator. He is the Advocate. He is the One, who made it possible for man once again to be in relationship with the Father.

Jesus alone made it possible for us to experience life as it had been in the beginning: one-on-one, face-to-face, heart-to-heart communication with the Father of Life. That is what humanity lost, and that is what Jesus' gift is to all of humanity. That is why the Cross changed everything on this planet: past, present and future. That event has no equal in all of history. That is what this book called The Revelation of Jesus is supposed to be about, rather than what it has become: "A riddle, wrapped in a mystery, inside an enigma."[45]

Read Hebrews Chapters 9 and 10, which talk of Jesus performing the duties of both sacrifice and High Priest.

7

Covenants

JESUS INTRODUCES HIMSELF:

"I am Alpha and Omega, Beginning and End"

Revelation 1:8a

It is safe to say the majority of today's Revelation readers take this to mean Jesus was there at the creation of the universe and start of the human race, and He will be there when life on this planet ceases to exist. True as that statement is, I don't think that is what He is talking about in this context.

Let's consider how the first-century readers may have processed the meaning of that introduction. To do that we must look at the significance of covenant.

What Is a Covenant?

The best example of a covenant we have in the West is marriage; two people with strengths and gifts to offer—as well as having limitations and desires unable to be fulfilled without a partner—enter into a legal agreement, joining together to help one another fulfill those desires. Each brings to the bargaining table all that they are and all they are not. The partnership they create and legally bind themselves to changes the course of their lives. When the Bible is referred to as a love letter, it is understood to be so, only through the concept of covenant. God, who knows our needs and understands our limitations, offers to meet those needs while conceding those limitations.

Any person attempting to read the Bible and makes it as far as Leviticus, has been introduced to this concept numerous times. A quick concordance search shows us that *covenant* is a major player in Jewish history and appears to be *the* way (following the garden debacle) in which God was able to continue to be an integral part of His created humanity.

What do Adam, Noah, Abraham, Moses, David and Jesus all have in common? They said *yes* to God's offer of covenant partnership, and in doing so, helped introduce another, previously unknown, facet of God's character in the earth. This is the way God has painstakingly established Himself in the history of His creation.

We know this because of the names by which the Lord reveals himself when we read the Biblical account of His interaction with humanity. At first God is simply known as Elohiym. Genesis 1 uses this name when referring to the God of Creation. In Genesis 2 we are invited to know Him more intimately.

Think of it like this. If you were to meet me on a busy sidewalk and notice that I dropped something, you could get my attention by saying,

"Hey, lady!"

That would thin out roughly half of the sidewalk walkers. If that didn't work, you could narrow the criteria by observation.

"Lady, with the purple coat…"

Assuming that works, I would graciously say, "Thank you! My name is Debi."

To which, the common response is, "Nice to meet you, Debi, my name is____."

I am no longer just a lady bumbling along on the sidewalk of life. I now have a name, you know that I am—although clumsy—not deaf. And,-I hope, you come to recognize me as a person capable of expressing appreciation.

So back to Genesis Chapters 1 and 2. The account of God's seven-step process in creating the universe is equivalent to the impersonal, "Hey, lady." Then, He introduces Himself in a more intimate way in verse 4 of Chapter 2.

"These are the generations of the heavens and of the earth, when they were created, in the day that the LORD God made the earth and the heavens"

Genesis 2:4

LORD God. Jehovah God. The Existing One God. The I AM that I AM God. The I Will Be what I Will Be God. What we are shown in Genesis Chapter 2 is a more intimate look at a more intimate work. Like a modern, abstract painting, the picture we are given in Genesis Chapter 1 uses broad strokes with broad meanings. Genesis Chapter 2 introduces us to a meticulous watercolor artist whose work is so precise that it is mistaken for a photograph.

Let's look at that verse again. Notice the order of the words: heaven and earth had been created, whereas earth and heaven are made. It's as if this verse serves as the apex. Were you to fold the two accounts in half, the crease would fall in the middle of 'whereas.' The accounts become mirror images of one another, not exact copies, but valuable for enhancing the rich depth and meanings that go unnoticed when a counterbalance is not present.

The implication is that after establishing the physical universe the LORD God set into motion the principles necessary for earth to know the glory of Heaven. Or this might be an opportunity to experiment with that punctuation thing we discussed earlier. What happens if the verse is divided into two sentences? It might read:

These are the generations of the heavens and the earth when they were created.

In the day the LORD God made the earth and heavens....

Either way, we are to recognize a significant difference in the narrative when Jehovah God stepped onto the stage and into the hearts of His created. Genesis Chapter 1 is big and impersonal. Genesis Chapter 2 is intimate and holy. Genesis Chapter 1 deals with the physical and scientific. Genesis Chapter 2 with the spiritual and relational: the realm of covenant.

From this introductory name we are graciously invited to know Him in even greater familiarity as He continues to reconnect with His creation, one covenant at a time. He is in:

- Genesis 22 —Jehovah Jirah, the Lord Who is provider and provision
- Exodus 15—Jehovah Rophe, the Lord Who is health and healer
- Exodus 17—Jehovah Nissi, the Lord Who is victorious and victory

- Leviticus Chapters 20, 21 and 22—Jehovah Mckeddesh, the Lord Who is sanctifier and makes holy
- Judges 6—Jehovah Shalom, the Lord Who is peace
- Psalms 23—Jehovah Rohi, the Lord Who is my shepherd
- Jeremiah 23 and 33—Jehovah Tsidkenu, the Lord Who is righteous and is our righteousness
- Ezekiel 48—Jehovah Shammah, the Lord Who is there overflowing within and upon

The Covenant of Man's Redemption Begins – It's a long, winding road

In Genesis we see that God is looking for a person worthy and willing to enter into an eternal, partnership with a man, who would dedicate his own life and the lives of all his decedents to this global cause. He found that willingness in a man named Abram. Granted there was some work that needed to be done, but God had already spent 2,000 years in the search, what's a few more decades?

WHAT DID AN ANCIENT COVENANT CEREMONY LOOK LIKE?

Genesis Chapter 15 gives us that answer. We get to read what happened at the ceremony when God established Abram and his descendants as legal owners of a portion of land.

> *⁹ "And He said to him, Bring to Me a heifer three years old, a she-goat three years old, a ram three years old, a turtledove, and a young pigeon. ¹⁰ And he brought Him all these and cut them down the middle [into halves] and laid each half opposite the other; but the birds he did not divide. ¹¹ And when the birds of prey swooped down upon the carcasses, Abram drove them away... ¹⁷ ...When the sun had gone down and a [thick] darkness had come on, behold, a smoking oven and a flaming torch passed between those pieces."*
>
> Genesis 15:9-17

One party (Abram) was responsible to bring to the ceremony certain elements. In this case it was the animals. He prepared them for the ceremony; the three large animals were split in half, their flesh splayed and their blood spilled. The two small birds remained whole.

After Abram prepared the animals for the ceremony, he had to stand guard over them. Even then scavenger birds were a determined lot and not easily deterred. The Lord enters the scene, and He is described as a smoking furnace and a burning torch,[46] walking in a series of figure eights (the infinity sign) between and among the opened flesh, mingling the blood of the sacrificed animals all together.

THE COVENANT OF REDEMPTION IS INITIATED

Would John's congregations in the cities of Asia Minor have known about this event? Absolutely! They were as familiar with it as we are with the stories of Christ's birth and crucifixion.

As important as the property-ownership covenant was, there is a covenant of much greater interest to our study of Revelation. It is The Covenant of Redemption, and we read about it in Genesis Chapter 17. In this covenant Abram gets his own skin in the game, and he is given a new name—a name that identifies and joins him to the One with Whom he has entered the covenant. Much like a bride in our Western culture takes her husband's name as her own; Jehovah God gives Abram and his wife, Sarai a portion of His name: ah. Abram is now Abraham, and Sarai is now Sarah.

This partnership opened the way for the Lord God Jehovah to implement His plan for humanity's redemption. It was His plan to redeem us from the confines of the state we had created through our surrender to the enemy at the fall in the garden. The fulfillment of that magnificent plan is what John was honored to witness and record, which gives us the honor of seeing it as well.

In these letters to the churches of Asia Minor, the Lord is reminding the people of the powerful position they are authorized to walk in as His joint-heirs. Because He so graciously included us (you and I) as benefactors of His covenant, we too are legal heirs.

Unlike the Old Covenant, which was a contract between God and the people of Israel-the New Covenant is NOT a contract between two parties—(one of which is absolutely guaranteed to fail). Instead, it is based on an oath made by God to Himself. By doing so, He designed a failsafe plan to ensure our success. What a phenomenal work of genius! We will be exploring the depths of that plan throughout this entire study. Trust me; you're going to love it.

"Men swear by someone greater than themselves, and the oath confirms what is said and puts an end to all argument. [17] Because God wanted to make the unchanging nature of his purpose very clear to the heirs of what was promised, he

confirmed it with an oath. [18] *God did this so that, by two unchangeable things in which it is impossible for God to lie, we who have fled to take hold of the hope offered to us may be greatly encouraged.* [19]*We have this hope as an anchor for the soul, firm and secure.*"

Hebrews 6: 16-19

This oath, which God swore by Himself, is based on these two facts:

    a. God cannot lie

    b. God is the highest authority (He swore by Himself)

PUTTING THE PIECES TOGETHER

Reading the first three chapters of Revelation from a covenant perspective, we see why it was necessary for God to have this event recorded for all future generations to read. Why? Because this single event has changed the entire course of human history. If the garden/fruit/tree incident had far-reaching ramifications, doesn't it stand to reason what was accomplished on that Cross just outside of Jerusalem should at least rival, if not eclipse, those in the garden? I do. I believe the Cross of Christ changed *everything*!

1. Reread Revelation 1:1-20. Here John describes receiving the commission from Heaven to record this history-changing event. What does he see that reminds us of the covenant ceremony described in Genesis 15?
   a. The smoking oven
   b. Flaming torch
   c. Walking among a flesh-and-blood offering

John records seeing in this covenant ceremony: the Lord Jesus Christ, dressed in priestly garments, as the smoking furnace (feet as fine brass as if they burned in a furnace) and holding (as one would a torch), in His right hand, seven stars.

Chapters 2 and 3 of Revelation describe in detail what the Lord observes as He walks in, around, and among the churches mingling all they are with all He is. He sees all that they are and all that they are not, and He offers all that He is to these living sacrifices, that they might enjoy and experience all that is now made available should they choose to agree to the terms offered in this New Covenant relationship. Popular, current interpretations of this event have viewed this as an indictment against the individual congregations. Were that the case, what difference is there between pre and post Cross? Essentially none. With this idea in mind, read:

- Matthew 26:28
- Mark 14:24
- Luke 22:20
- 1 Corinthians 11:25

These verses all describe the same incident: Jesus instructing us on the real meaning behind the symbolic celebration of Passover.

Jeremiah 31:31-34 (written approximately 627 years before the time of Christ) gives us one of the clearest descriptions of God's promised New Covenant.

Hebrews 12:22-29 tells us that Jesus is the agent of this New Covenant.

Romans 12:1 tells us to be living sacrifices.

The Cross marks the moment on the earth and Heaven, when the Old Covenant was fulfilled. It also marks the moment on earth and Heaven, when the New Covenant began.

IF NOT AN INDICTMENT, WHAT?

75

Just like God, revealing more and more of Himself through each of the covenant relationships He entered into with man; Jesus reveals to us His covenant attributes as well. Interesting to note that all of these are found in the Gospel of John (the same John, who wrote Revelation):

- John 6—I AM The Bread of Life
- John 8—I AM The Light
- John 10—I AM The Door and The Shepherd
- John 11—I AM The Resurrection and The Life
- John 14 —I AM The Way, The Truth, The Life
- John 15—I AM The Vine
- Revelation 1—I AM Alpha and Omega

    I AM The First and The Last.

    I AM He Who Lives, was dead.

    I AM Alive Forevermore.

None of this makes any real sense unless viewed from a legal perspective and by comprehending all humanity lost by rejecting God's ways and devising, instead, a system of laws that appeal to human sensibility.[47]

Do you take this man to be your lawful savior, redeemer and lord?

I do!

8

History Lesson

Accepting the crucial difference between Eastern and Western perspective is vital if we are ever going to come close to grasping the message being communicated in this document. One neon example of differing concepts is the idea of progress.

The Past Is Visible; The Future Is Not

Western tendency has been to take stabs at interpreting this book futuristically. While there may be merit in that, might it be more beneficial to adopt a Hebrew mindset? One must look behind, to the past, to gain a clear understanding of the present and the future.

Go forward by looking back is the way of Hebrew/Eastern thought. Think about rowing a boat. The rower faces backward, looking at where they have been and unable to see where they are heading.

In John's letter to the churches found in Revelation Chapters 2 and 3, specific issues with which those congregations struggled (and we continue to deal with today) are addressed. A comprehensive game plan for overcoming those hindrances is given, as well. The reality of the Cross, is we are joint heirs with Jesus, and all that He is and all that He accomplished is intended for all of us.

The conventional Western microscopic interpretation has led to fragmented conclusions. For this study it is best to use a tool designed to show the big picture—a telescope. We need to see where we've been, how we got where we are, and gives us the coordinates for where we are going. The telescope we will use is the historical record of human existence contained in the Hebrew Torah.

This approach will allow us to see how the individual pieces might fit more cohesively in the whole. We do this by pulling back from our tendency to dissect elements. We will, instead, read the work as a single unit, rather than a collection of individual parts. It is, after all, a letter containing a message, not a dictionary of unrelated words.

The people John is addressing were among the first to embrace the covenant of the Cross. They were not unlike the pilgrims of our nation's history, who set out to establish something that had never been done before. The first-century Christ Followers set out to build their lives on the belief that the Cross of Christ had redeemed humanity from the law of sin and death. They believed that Christ had made them free and that they were no longer subject to the universal dictates established because of humanity's fall. They believed that because of the Cross Satan was no longer their warden. Jesus Christ was now their King! The new kingdom was, as Jesus had described, a spiritual kingdom, realized and experienced in the hearts of humanity. If anyone had ever been charged with the task of moving forward, these people were. And if ever a people needed to have a clear image of the past to aid them in their journey forward, these people did.

John, within the context of their current reality, fashioned a message to help them see the big picture, reminding them of where man had been and the direction they needed to go. He did that by sprinkling the message with words that sparked images of the past, images with which his congregation was very familiar.

The message contains a golden thread that is clearly visible when approached from the look-behind-to-move-forward perspective. Woven in the seven individual messages to the individual congregations is humanity's 4,000-year corporate history. It begins with the fall and ends with a warning to all who wish to walk with God in His Kingdom today.

The Telescopic Overview

EPHESUS

REMEMBER THE REASON

#1 Revelation 2:5 & 7 tells us:

Remember from whence you have fallen.

Repent (change your mind concerning this issue).

The ability to eat from the tree (source) of life, which is in the center of God's Paradise (an honor that had been lost as a result of the fall) will be reinstated.

82

The first message to the church is a reminder of the reason man was in need of redemption—humanity had fallen into the trap laid by the enemy. They were cut off from God; Who Alone Is The Source of human purpose and existence. Until that reality is fully comprehended, the human mind will continue to play the I'm-not-that-bad game, which keeps us from ever acknowledging our need for redemption in the first place.

SMYRNA

SEPARATION FROM GOD IS DEATH

#2 Revelation 2:8-11 is a reminder that the result of man's fall was death. Death being defined by God's terms, which is separation from the Life of God.

That separation plunged man into an existence of imprisonment, tribulation and death.

PERGAMOS

FAITHFUL REMNANT

#3 Revelation 2:12-17 reminds us of the struggle to keep the Jewish nation alive and walking in the ways of Truth, undefiled by deception, idolatry, human tendency and perversion. The fact is that this had to be accomplished smack dab in the middle of Satan's domain, under his dictates and governing laws.

God's phenomenal plan was implemented and fulfilled in and through Christ Jesus, in spite of all the enemy's efforts throughout history to destroy the Jewish nation. A remnant had always remained faithful to the promise God made to fix the mess man had created. This remnant trusted God and His ways on pure faith alone, because the world's reality has always been completely contrary to the Truth of God.

THYATIRA
OUR REDEEMER ARRIVES

#4 Revelation 2:18-29 The Son of God, humanity's redeeming sacrifice arrives on the earth.

Christ Himself entered that realm of imprisonment, tribulation and death and in so doing reestablished Life in humanity. He accomplished this by fulfilling the demands of the laws that governed sin and death, thereby conquering death on mankind's behalf.

We are familiar with how God accomplished this amazing feat. The Savior of all mankind snuck onto the planet and into the fabric of humanity as an unimpressive infant, born in a barn surrounded by insignificance. He set out to fulfill His mission, which demanded He live a sinless life, die a sinner's death, pay the ransom demanded by the laws that then governed humanity concerning sin and death, descend into the depths of hell and from that horrific place continue to believe in God's plan.

Then He was to be raised from death, becoming the firstborn from the dead and present Himself at the court of Heaven as an adequate sacrifice for man's redemption.

An absolutely brilliant plan, flawlessly executed!

SARDIS

CREATOR AND CREATION UNITE

#5 Revelation 3:1-6 Because our God is so completely over-the-top in love with you, and delighted with Jesus' epic accomplishment and desires nothing but the best for our lives, He enters the fabric of humanity by giving us Himself—by way of His Spirit—to reside in the hearts of all who choose to receive Him. This event, promised through the ages, was realized in the earth following Christ's departure. It is recorded in the book of Acts, Chapter 2.

God's Spirit arrived on the earth following Christ's success in completing His mission, and Christ's sacrifice had been judged as completely adequate for redeeming mankind from the judgment held against them for the previous 4,000 years. Righteousness is restored. God can again commune with His dearly loved creation.

Only when the human heart has grasped these historical realities will it be capable of walking in the Kingdom of God, which is illustrated in the message to the sixth church on John's list.

PHILADELPHIA
TREE OF LIFE

#6 Revelation 3:7-13 Contains the message of what it looks like when humans commit their lives to advancing the Kingdom of God by walking in the principles of that Kingdom: righteousness, peace and joy in God's Holy Spirit.

Believing that I am righteous because I have been given Christ Jesus' righteousness puts me back to the same place enjoyed by Adam and Eve before the fall, where we had set our sights on playing gods, building our own kingdoms built on human sensibility, and selling our species into slavery to the law of sin and death.

Peace comes from knowing that I am righteous because of Christ Jesus and His accomplishment at the Cross, that the one who had been building the case and accusing me in the court of heaven has been forever silenced and that there is only peace between me and my Father.

Joy is not an emotion. It is a spiritual reality, and it is where strength is found. Because God's Spirit now resides in me and is my ever-present companion, I have an unlimited source of strength to inspire and motivate my decisions and empower my life.

Message number six also explains how God's promise to David—that his family would sit on a throne and rule eternally—was fulfilled. As a descendant of King David, Jesus Christ satisfied the criteria and fulfills that promise.

This also describes the current equivalent to the Tree of Life we see in Genesis. All those same elements are again in play today because Christ has reconciled us back into the presence of God. We are invited to know Him, access His wisdom, ask questions and receive answers—in short, to be in relationship with our Father. And like Adam and Eve, we are presented with two choices. This one, illustrated in message number six, leads to life. The other, described in message number seven, leads to death.

LAODICEA

TREE THAT BRINGS DEATH

#7 Revelation 3:14-22 This is humanity's current equivalent to the tree that leads to death.

The temptation we are faced with is to mix the laws of sin and death, which governed humanity before the Cross, together with the laws of grace and peace implemented by God through the Cross of Christ. To make this choice is to nullify the Cross and make Christ's life and sacrifice of no effect.

It is all Christ or nothing at all. It is not a little bit of Jesus and God's redemption plan and a little bit of my flesh effort. That is what happened in the garden, when man chose against God's plan and decided to establish their own ideas into laws—a little bit of obedience and a lot of what makes sense to me.

Christ is King, and He establishes the laws that govern His Kingdom, and there is no room for pre-Cross concepts of how to achieve righteousness.

What if the Cross Changed Everything?

9

Church Challenges

This chapter is dedicated to the seven churches of Asia Minor and follows a pattern for each of the churches addressed: recipient identified, sender identified, assessment given, course of action prescribed with warnings for failure to implement and promises for succeeding to do so.[48]

MESSAGE #1

There came a time in history, when humans were completely separated and cut off from gaining access to Life.[49] God became a memory. Humanity plunged into the darkness that comes from rejecting His ways as we sought to establish a life based on our own sense of right and wrong, with no way back to how it was originally intended to be.

What did the Cross of Christ do? It is revealed to us in the message to Ephesus. Jesus restored access to the Tree of Life, which is firmly planted in the center of God's delight.

"Unto the angel of the church of Ephesus write: These things saith he that holdeth the seven stars in his right hand, who walketh in the midst of the seven golden candlesticks;
[2] I know thy works, and thy labour, and thy patience, and how thou canst not bear them which are evil: and thou hast tried them which say they are apostles, and are not, and hast found them liars: [3] And hast borne, and hast patience, and for my name's sake hast laboured, and hast not fainted. [4] Nevertheless I have somewhat against thee, because thou hast left thy first love. [5] Remember therefore from whence thou art fallen, and repent, and do the first works; or else I will come unto thee quickly, and will remove thy candlestick out of his place, except thou repent. But this thou hast, that thou hatest the deeds of the Nicolaitanes, which I also hate.
[7] He that hath an ear, let him hear what the Spirit saith unto the churches; To him that overcometh will I give to eat of the tree of life, which is in the midst of the paradise of God.

Revelation 2:1-7

APPEARED: This congregation appeared busy and in-dustrious. They recognized legitimate ministers from illegiti-mate and were patient and long-suffering.

WHAT JESUS SAW: They had become 'duty-bound' and lost sight of their fundamental purpose: to be in relationship with the Father and let the love they enjoyed motivate their lives. They became like Cain, attempting to impress God with their efforts and their ideas of what needed to be counted as righteous. Bad idea.

THE COVENANT NAME OF JESUS: He is Lord, Holder, Keeper and assessor of the church

THE TRUTH THEY NEEDED: These things were not their responsibilities and that they were not the "church police."

PRESCRIBED COURSE OF ACTION: Remember what it was like when they began their walk and work with Jesus—when the work was because they knew they were loved—not because they were busy and right. And the solution for this malady? Repentance. Repent simply means to change your thinking. In this case the thinking that needed to be changed is the way they had come to think regarding the purpose of their redemption. Redemption doesn't qualify a person to sit in the seat of judgment. Repent from becoming self-righteous, and return to the first works, when their works were motivated purely from love.

CONSEQUENCE FOR FAILURE TO IMPLEMENT HIS CORRECTION: The church would quickly cease being a place of light, unable to show others the path of the Kingdom and light the way to the Father.

Reward **FOR OBEDIENCE:** Eat of the fruit of the Tree of Life in the paradise of God.

This first letter clearly refers to the first act of disobedience recorded in Genesis[50] by Adam and Eve in the Garden of Eden[51]. By choosing to consume the fruit of judgment (good and evil), rather than life, what happened? Their inner light, love and life immediately became dark. How do we know this? By looking at the fruit their lives produced: self-awareness, fear, blame, justification and a refusal to repent.

The first message to the church then remains the primary message to the church today. Recognize the danger of falling into the same pattern of destruction. They had enjoyed the pleasure of walking with God on the high road of love.

However, when the opportunity presented itself to step into a place of judgment and become like God—even for so noble-appearing a cause as blowing the whistle on false ministers and teachers of lies—they were in danger of falling for the same lie that had plunged humanity into the darkness in the first place!

We have a gracious, empowering God, which is why He instructs us and shows us the way out of the situations we get ourselves in. The way to navigate out of this trap—the same one all humans have fallen for—is a simple three-step plan: remember, repent, return—a plan our first ancestors refused to consider.

To embrace the deceptive notion that I know what is good and right, bad and evil is diametrically opposed to the things that support life. That's why we are given the picture of a garden that has two trees, one that produces life-giving, life-sustaining fruit.[52] The other tree produces fruit that feeds and promotes death.

MESSAGE #2

[8] And unto the angel of the church in Smyrna write; These things saith the first and the last, which was dead,

95

and is alive; ^{9} I know thy works, and tribulation, and poverty,(but thou art rich) and I know the blasphemy of them which say they are Jews, and are not, but are the synagogue of Satan. ^{10} Fear none of those things which thou shalt suffer: behold, the devil shall cast some of you into prison, that ye may be tried; and ye shall have tribulation ten days: be thou faithful unto death, and I will give thee a crown of life.

^{11} He that hath an ear, let him hear what the Spirit saith unto the churches; He that overcometh shall not be hurt of the second death.

Revelation 2:8-11

APPEARED: Weak, powerless, persecuted

WHAT JESUS SAW: The truth—They were rich

THE COVENANT name OF JESUS: The One Who conquered death, removed their guilt, paid their penalty

THE TRUTH they NEEDED: no longer guilty, the penalty had been paid, what it means to be a new creation in Christ.

Prescription: Stop believing the blasphemes (anti-Christ) teachings of those who insist they remain under the confines and former truths of the Jewish laws. Stop being controlled by fear.

Be faithful to "the" death (establish their faith on what Jesus accomplished in His death, burial and resurrection). To do so will crown them (authority will come upon them) with life.

CONSEQUENCE FOR FAILURE: They will continue to believe the former covenant, feel obligated to pay the penalties and suffer the punishment of their sin. They will die.

REWARD FOR OBEDIENCE: Not be hurt by the second death.

MESSAGE #3

[12] **And to the angel of the church in Pergomos write; These things saith he which hath the sharp sword with two edges;** [13] **I know thy works, and where thou dwellest, even where Satan's seat is: and thou holdest fast my name, and hast not denied my faith, even in those days wherein Antipas was my faithful martyr, who was slain among you, where Satan dwelleth.**

[14] **But I have a few things against thee, because thou hast there them that hold the doctrine of Balaam, who taught Balac to cast a stumbling-block before the children of Israel, to eat things sacrificed unto idols, and to commit fornication.** [15] **So hast thou also them that hold the doctrine of the Nicolaitanes, which thing I hate.** [16] **Repent; or else I**

will come unto thee quickly, and will fight against them with the sword of my mouth.

[17] He that hath an ear, let him hear what the Spirit saith unto the churches; To him that overcometh will I give to eat of the hidden manna, and will give him a white stone, and in the stone a new name written, which no man knoweth saving he that receiveth it.

Revelation 2:12-17

APPEARED: Survivors in the midst of the enemy's camp: strong, steadfast, and unshakeable.

WHAT JESUS SAW: They tolerated and left unchecked those who would diminish the value of the Kingdom by sleeping around and participating in other things that are forbidden— feeding off of the types of things used in the worship—or honoring of false gods.

THE COVENANT NAME OF JESUS: He alone is the wielder of Truth—He speaks truth and is able to, with His words.

THE TRUTH THEY NEEDED: Truth of God's Word separates the authentic from the perverse, the thoughts and the intents, the soul and the spirit.

PRESCRIPTION: Repent themselves

CONSEQUENCE FOR FAILURE: Jesus will, Himself, oppose them. Their lies and perversions are in direct opposition to His truth.

REWARD FOR OBEDIENCE: Give to eat of the manna that is hidden, a "not guilty" sentence and a new identity.

MESSAGE #4

¹⁸ And unto the angel of the church in Thyatira write; These things saith the Son of God, who hath his eyes like unto a flame of fire, and his feet are like fine brass;
¹⁹ I know thy works, and charity, and service, and faith, and thy patience, and thy works; and the last to be more than the first.
²⁰ Notwithstanding I have a few things against thee, because thou sufferest that woman Jezebel, which calleth herself a prophetess, to teach and to seduce my servants to commit fornication, and to eat things sacrificed unto idols.
²¹ And I gave her space to repent of her fornication; and she repented not. ²² Behold, I will cast her into a bed, and them that commit adultery with her into great tribulation, except they repent of their deeds. ²³ And I will kill her children with death; and all the churches shall know that I am he which searcheth the reins and hearts: and I will give unto every one of you according to your works. ²⁴ But unto you I say, and unto the rest in Thyatira, as many as have not this doctrine, and which have not known the depths of

Satan, as they speak; I will put upon you none other burden. [25] But that which ye have already hold fast till I come.

[26] And he that overcometh, and keepeth my works unto the end, to him will I give power over the nations:[27] And he shall rule them with a rod of iron; as the vessels of a potter shall they be broken to shivers: even as I received of my Father. [28] And I will give him the morning star.

[29] He that hath an ear, let him hear what the Spirit saith unto the churches.

Revelation 2:18-29

APPEARED: Charitable, service oriented, patient and growing in works

WHAT JESUS SAW: They permitted a false teacher to corrupt the people with teachings that encouraged mingling of false religions with "The Way" and to incorporate the worship methods used in false/idol worship with the worship of God.

THE COVENANT NAME OF JESUS: Son of God, the only sacrifice

THE TRUTH THEY NEEDED: That He alone is the one who was purified and worthy of worship—no other! And that

He alone is the Knower, the Seer, the Discerner, the Worthy Sacrifice.

When the Word speaks of adultery and offspring or children in this context, it is not referring to a physical/sexual act, nor is the Lord threatening to kill children! He is talking about the mingling of His Truth and the worship of the One True God with the worship practices that honor false gods. God is not keen on sharing your worship with any other god. That is why worship is often likened to the intimacy shared between husband and wife. No one else allowed! On this there is no negotiating.

If and when a person comes to realize their error, and repent, the Lord, great in mercy and compassion, loving kindness and grace steps into the places He is invited to and begins the process of separating truth from lie, false from real, thoughts from intent, soul from spirit. These are the 'children' produced from the time spent entertaining the enemy and coupling false with the truth already resident in your heart.

PRESCRIPTION: There are 2—one for those whose hearts were defiled and another for those, who did not fall into the false teaching.

For those whose hearts received and reproduced this mutation—repent and grant the Lord access to their inner life—let Him, who knows the thoughts and the intents—do the work necessary to separate Truth from lie.

For those whose belief system was not adulterated by the effects of the false teaching—they are to allow time for Jesus to do and accomplish Himself—the work necessary in the hearts of those, who were affected. The unadulterated folks are—with authority and strength[53]—to care for, feed, lead (as a shepherd) those people Christ is working on.

There was a woman who taught in this church. The issue isn't her gender. Nor is it her name, methods or tactics. The issue was her false message and the fact that the authentic leaders of the congregation allowed her to continue polluting the people with her false ideas.

The Lord tells us that He confronted her, gave her time and opportunity to turn away from what she was doing, but she refused. However, some who had been 'sleeping in her bed' did want to turn and rid themselves of their spiritual indiscretions. This is where the Lord Jesus announces that He Himself will perform the delicate surgery necessary to separate His truth from lies. He warns that it will be time consuming, and for those who are not in need of His special surgical skills— they are given the responsibility to minister, care for, feed and lead these formerly deceived and disillusioned ones.

CONSEQUENCE FOR FAILURE: No light, life or truth.

REWARD FOR OBEDIENCE: Authority and power over the nations, and the Morning Star.

MESSAGE #5

And unto the angel of the church in Sardis write; These things saith he that hath the seven Spirits of God, and the seven stars; I know thy works, that thou hast a name that thou livest, and art dead.
 ² Be watchful, and strengthen the things which remain, that are ready to die: for I have not found thy works perfect before God. ³ Remember therefore how thou hast received and heard, and hold fast, and repent. If therefore thou shalt not watch, I will come on thee as a thief, and thou shalt not know what hour I will come upon thee.
 ⁴ Thou hast a few names even in Sardis which have not defiled their garments; and they shall walk with me in white: for they are worthy.
 ⁵ He that overcometh, the same shall be clothed in white raiment; and I will not blot out his name out of the

book of life, but I will confess his name before my Father, and before his angels.

^{6} He that hath an ear, let him hear what the Spirit saith unto the churches.

Revelation 3:1-6

APPEARED: Alive and working

WHAT JESUS SAW: They declared their works to be alive—but they were dead (remember, dead works are the works humans do in an effort to earn salvation).

THE COVENANT NAME OF JESUS: That Jesus is The One with the Perfected (completed and viable-reproducible) Spirit of God.

THE TRUTH THEY NEEDED: Jesus, is the One with the message for the church—it's His message, not theirs or what they can come up with.

PRESCRIPTION: Remember how salvation was obtained, by hearing the word and receiving (passionately grabbing hold of) and not letting it go. Repent of what they had become and come to believe.

Remember that Jesus is the Groom[54]—the people are His betrothed. Their responsibility, while He is away preparing a place for them, is to make themselves ready and remain in watchful anticipation of His return.

Know and learn from those among them who have put on the Righteousness of Christ and walk in His righteousness rather than their own standard of righteousness.

CONSEQUENCE FOR FAILURE: If they do not prepare themselves—by putting on the garment that He has provided for them—(His Righteousness) then they will not be permitted to enter into the marriage to which they were most certainly invited.

REWARD FOR OBEDIENCE: Made righteous, name not blotted out of the book of life, adopted as His own in the court of Heaven.

MESSAGE #6

[7]"**And to the angel of the church in Philadelphia write; These things saith he that is holy, he that is true, he that hath the key of David, he that openeth, and no man shutteth; and shutteth, and no man openeth;** [8]**I know thy works: behold, I have set before thee an open door, and no**

man can shut it: for thou hast a little strength, and hast kept my word, and hast not denied my name. [9] Behold, I will make them of the synagogue of Satan, which say they are Jews, and are not, but do lie; behold, I will make them to come and worship before thy feet, and to know that I have loved thee. [10] Because thou hast kept the word of my patience, I also will keep thee from the hour of temptation, which shall come upon all the world, to try them that dwell upon the earth.

[11] Behold, I come quickly: hold that fast which thou hast, that no man take thy crown. [12] Him that overcometh will I make a pillar in the temple of my God, and he shall go no more out: and I will write upon him the name of my God, and the name of the city of my God, which is new Jerusalem, which cometh down out of heaven from God: and I will write upon him my new name. [13] He that hath an ear, let him hear what the Spirit saith unto the churches."

Revelation 3:7-13

APPEARED: Insignificant—especially to the maintainers of the Old Covenant

WHAT JESUS SAW: A humble, worthy body of believers —Keepers and holders of all Jesus obtained

THE COVENANT NAME OF JESUS: Holy, True, Keeper of the Keys of the Tabernacle and reign of King David (a worshipper and one who had a hunger to pursue the heart of God).

THE TRUTH THEY NEEDED: Jesus is their everything. He leads and guides and strengthens

PRESCRIPTION: Hold fast—with strength, power and diligence the crown (authority) you walk in. Do not allow yourself to be tricked or duped out of believing that you are and walk in the Authority of the Kingdom.

CONSEQUENCE FOR FAILURE: Authority usurped, stolen

REWARD FOR OBEDIENCE: Be made a pillar in the sanctuary of God, never be put out of God's sanctuary. New name/identity.

MESSAGE #7

[14] **And unto the angel of the church of the Laodiceans write; These things saith the Amen, the faithful and true witness, the beginning of the creation of God;** [15] **I know thy works, that thou art neither cold nor hot: I would thou wert cold or hot.** [16] **So then because thou art**

lukewarm, and neither cold nor hot, I will spew thee out of my mouth.

[17] Because thou sayest, I am rich, and increased with goods, and have need of nothing; and knowest not that thou art wretched, and miserable, and poor, and blind, and naked: [18] I counsel thee to buy of me gold tried in the fire, that thou mayest be rich; and white raiment, that thou mayest be clothed, and that the shame of thy nakedness do not appear; and anoint thine eyes with eye salve, that thou mayest see. [19] As many as I love, I rebuke and chasten: be zealous therefore, and repent. [20] Behold, I stand at the door, and knock: if any man hear my voice, and open the door, I will come in to him, and will sup with him, and he with me.

[21] To him that overcometh will I grant to sit with me in my throne, even as I also overcame, and am set down with my Father in his throne.

[22] He that hath an ear, let him hear what the Spirit saith unto the churches.

Revelation 3:14-22

APPEARED: Neutral

WHAT JESUS SAW: A group that had so mingled the Old Covenant with the New Covenant and the standards of the world with the ideas of the Kingdom that they were completely powerless and ineffective—a group that didn't know Who He was, What He accomplished or what their purpose was. They were blind to truth, their situation, and their un-righteousness.

THE COVENANT NAME OF JESUS: That He had the final say—He calls the shots—

THE TRUTH THEY NEEDED: because He is the Creator of the plan it's His way—no other.

PRESCRIPTION: Pay the price necessary to obtain the robe of righteousness offered by Christ (repent—let go of their own ideas of how this is to be and work—can't have a mulligan stew standard of world values, Old Covenant values, personal values and a pinch of Kingdom values. It's all Christ or nothing. And they have to pay the price to see things the way the Lord sees them—again that price is paid by surrendering their view and opinion in exchange for His view and opinion.

CONSEQUENCE FOR FAILURE: Will not be able to hear the Lord knocking—will not open the door to Him—will not hear what He says to them—will not have a relationship with Him.

REWARD FOR OBEDIENCE: Be given a place in the throne room of heaven—seated next to the Lord.

It is not difficult to see that each of these ancient congregations face the same challenges we face today individually and collectively. There is not a single reward that I would choose to discount, nor can I deny not having struggled with the same things these first century Christians struggled with. When viewed in this manner, it is not beneficial to view these as some have suggested; eras or divisions of church history. That theory puts the warnings, prescriptions and rewards on a shelf too high for me to reach, to distant for me to embrace, and too foreign for me to validate.

10

Doors, Thrones, Scrolls & Seals

Has it ever struck you as odd that we have a permanent record–of the fall of man and the elements leading to the promise of humanity's redemption, but very little describing the culmination of that 4,000-year odyssey apart from a few verses and a couple of chapters sprinkled here and there? Why is that? Perhaps the better question to ask would be: Is that?

What if this document known as the Revelation of Jesus Christ describes the far-reaching effects of this phenomenal event? Remember our constant: What if the Cross changed everything?

After this I understood (or comprehended) and beheld the open door in Heaven and the voice, which I heard as a trumpet, speak with me. He said you ascended here—

to this place—and I will show you whatsoever things which must come[55] **as a result of these things.**

Revelation 4:1 (Author's translation).

What "Things" Are We Talking About?

We're talking about:

1. The initiation of the New Covenant, in which Jesus entered into a partnership with humanity, that John was called to witness and commissioned to record.
2. The cataclysmic effects His Cross had in and on every facet of life.

The greatest surprise to come from this study was in realizing John is describing the greatest event in all of human history! He has recorded the universe-altering events surrounding the Redemption of Man Covenant Ceremony—that moment in history where Jesus offers all He Is to all we are not and instructs John to send the document to the church. Why? Because the church—then and now—has something to offer: their physical presence. It is through human beings God's love is to be shown and multiplied and His Kingdom established in the earth. That is the partnership agreement.

The fact that this Book of Revelation has been grossly misunderstood, misinterpreted and consequently relegated to the obscure and irrelevant is absolutely heartbreaking. What have we lost because this treasure has remained buried in speculation and cloaked in mystery?

Again we will look at the covenant of marriage to illuminate the basic principles of this glorious partnership we have been invited to join. My marriage ceremony took place on November 29, 1980 at 1 PM. The laws that govern the behavior and expectations of an unmarried person were in place that morning. Following the ceremony those laws were no longer applicable.

As a married couple we'd agreed to walk together under a different set of laws. We put ourselves in a legal, binding agreement to be faithful to one another and exclude all others. That simple ceremony, as unspectacular and obscure as it may have been, is legal and binding. Did I feel different the moment after the I do? No. Did I feel like I was doing something wrong when we checked into the hotel to begin our honeymoon? Yes. A few, "repeat after me" statements, a couple of songs and a new piece of jewelry doesn't erase the life I lived before. It takes a little time to be comfortable with a new reality.

What does all this talk of marriage have to do with Revelation? Everything! Let's continue using this metaphor to look back to the Garden of Eden and the moment when humans set the course that separated them (and their posterity) from the Life of God.

In an obscure, unspectacular moment of time, humans chose to live a life governed by what appealed to their physical senses and reasoning abilities. By rejecting the truths of Life governed by Love and embracing the dichotomous concepts of an existence governed by good/evil, right/wrong, punish/pay the world quickly descended into fear and death—an existence ruled by the laws of sin and death.

After hi-jacking the authority that God had delegated to humanity, the evil, dictatorial ruler of that miserable, lifeless existence was certain he had all of humanity locked up tight in his 'iron clad' penal system.

Thank God (literally) for the 'dust-clad' design He had up His sleeve; those few ambiguous loopholes set the stage for the implementation of His magnificent plan.

Jesus has redeemed (paid the price to release us from our prison sentence) by becoming our sin, giving us the freedom and option to receive His righteousness, and marry our lives with the Spirit of Life. What a deal! The church is His Bride. Our Redeemer is not a friends-with-benefits partner. No, He is a covenant-relationship-for-life-eternal partner.

Back at the Throne

The door is standing open in heaven. Is this statement significant? To the 21st century Western mind, probably not, but might it say something to those first-century readers, who had lived under the law of sin and death, waiting and believing for God's promised Deliverer to step into history and change their lives for all eternity. To people familiar with what it was like to exist separated from the Life of God, familiar with the imagery of the Temple and the purpose of the rituals, to be told that the door now stands open is huge.

Remember the image of the tabernacle in Chapter Six? There were three access points to three separate areas:

- A gate leading to the outer court where sacrifices were made
- A door leading to the Holy Place

- A veil that separated that from The Holiest of All

THE DOOR IS STANDING OPEN

The place accessed through the door is the Holy Place. John says he sees God seated on the throne he sees through the open door to the throne room of God.

Think of our modern day courtrooms and the principal players:

- The Judge
- Lawyers
- Parties
- Witnesses
- Court Deputy
- Court Reporter

Now all that talk about legal documentation, court reporting and qualifying witnesses we discussed in Chapter Four begins to make sense. John has been summoned to the courtroom of Heaven to observe and report the greatest legal proceedings in the history of humanity.

Read Revelation Chapters 4 and 5. John describes what he sees and introduces us to the key players:

- The Holy, Just, Righteous Judge (God)
- Twenty-four Royal Righteous Elders (Lawyers)
- Four Earth Representatives (Witnesses)
- A Sea of Humanity (Party 1)
- Court Deputy (Angel)
- Court Reporter (John)

The case to be heard is written on a sealed scroll that rests on the Judge's hand.

"And I saw in the right hand of him that sat on the throne a book written within and on the backside, sealed with seven seals.
^{2} And I saw a strong angel (court deputy) proclaiming with a loud voice, Who is worthy to open the book, and to loose^{56} the seals thereof?"

Revelation 5:1-2

This image of a scroll written on the inside and the outside is an interesting bit of Jewish- culture-meets-Roman-law. When a Jewish person became indebted and were forced to sell either property or self into indentured servitude, all that information was recorded on the inside of a scroll. On the outside of that scroll was written the qualification demands for redeeming the property and persons. In Hebrew culture, strict guidelines were followed to ensure the land God had given to one tribe remained in that same family line. These guidelines are known as the Law of the Near Kinsman—or The Kinsman Redeemer Law.[57] It was the duty and obligation of this man's brother(s) to redeem the property and persons of his family. If a brother was unwilling or unable, the next near kinsman approached would be uncles. The third group on the list would be cousins and last would be any male relative.

Similarly humanity found itself duped and indebted to the law of sin and death. The qualification demands placed on anyone wishing to redeem mankind from the enslavement was unimaginably high considering John's reaction in Revelation 5:

[3] **"And no man in heaven, nor in earth, neither under the earth, was able to open the book, neither to look thereon.**
[4] **And I wept much, because no man was found worthy to open and to read the book, neither to look thereon."**
[5] **"And one of the elders saith unto me, Weep not: behold, the Lion of the tribe of Judah, the Root of David, hath prevailed to open the book, and to loose the seven seals thereof."**
[6] **And I beheld, and, lo, in the midst of the throne and of the four beasts, and in the midst of the elders, stood a Lamb as it had been slain, having seven horns and seven**

eyes, which are the seven Spirits of God sent forth into all the earth.

[7] And he (The Lamb) came and took the book out of the right hand of him that sat upon the throne.

Revelation 5:3-7

Just imagine it. John weeping over the desperate condition of humanity, but then something extraordinary happens. Into the courtroom of heaven enters the Sacrificial Lamb *and* the Lion of the Tribe of Judah. The two are beautifully rolled into one—Jesus Christ! John is witness to God's magnificent plan's unfolding.

Jesus takes the scroll inscribed with all we had lost.

[8] And when he had taken the book, the four beasts and four and twenty elders fell down before the Lamb, having every one of them harps, and golden vials full of odours, which are the prayers of saints.

Revelation 5:8

The witnesses for earth, and the twenty-four experts of the laws of heaven were given a new song to sing which declared:

"Thou art worthy to take the book, and to open the seals thereof: for thou wast slain, and hast redeemed us to

119

God by thy blood out of every kindred, and tongue, and people, and nation; [10] And hast made us unto our God kings and priests: and we shall reign on the earth.

Revelation 5:9,10

Everyone present in the courtroom agreed that Jesus met the prescribed criteria.

[11] And I beheld, and I heard the voice of many angels round about the throne and the beasts and the elders: and the number of them was ten thousand times ten thousand, and thousands of thousands—"

Revelation 5:11

All that humanity had surrendered was written on that scroll. The Near Kinsman has come forward to redeem what had been relinquished. What was written on that scroll? God knew, Jesus knew, the twenty-four Elders knew, Earth's Representatives knew, and every Angel of Heaven knew. And John recorded it so that we too might know:

[12] Saying with a loud voice, "Worthy is the Lamb that was slain to receive power, and riches, and wisdom, and strength, and honour, and glory, and blessing."

Revelation 5:12

Jesus received all that the enemy had gained access to and humanity had lost:

- Power
- Riches
- Wisdom
- Strength
- Honor
- Glory
- Blessing

Every messenger of heaven (Angels) and the representatives of the earth (the four Creatures around the throne) and experts of the law (twenty-four Elders) declare from heaven over all creation:

[13] And every creature which is in heaven, and on the earth, and under the earth, and such as are in the sea, and all that are in them, heard I saying, Blessing, and honour, and glory, and power, be unto him that sitteth upon the throne, and unto the Lamb forever and ever.

[14] And the four beasts said, Amen. And the four and twenty elders fell down and worshipped him that liveth forever and ever.

Revelation 5:13, 14

Every created entity agrees with the heavenly declaration. The earth's representatives say "amen," and in doing so,

121

acknowledge the right of this truth to be established on earth as it is in heaven.

The elders, recognizing the brilliancy of God's glorious plan, are in absolute awe of the Planner and the execution of this cosmic game-changer.

THE SEVEN SEALS

The mention of these seals nods to Roman influence in the imagery. John's first-century readers would have easily recognized a document with seven seals as a legal document,[58] often a will. Under Roman law when a sealed document was to be opened a majority of the original witnesses—who would have pressed their mark into the wax or clay used to seal the document—had to be present when the scroll was opened and presented for redemption.[59] These witnesses were called signatories. In the case of a seven-sealed document at least four of those witnesses had to make their way to the court-room.

11

Witnesses Summoned

In Revelation 5 Things Get Interesting

Here's the picture: John is in the throne room of Heaven. God is seated on the throne. Most of the principal players of a classic-courtroom scene are assembled, and the case being considered is of universal interest and affects all of humanity. Jesus is present as the conquering Lion of the Tribe of Judah and as the Sacrificial Lamb to claim—as the Near Kinsman Redeemer—His rights to access whatever is written on that sealed scroll.

All those in attendance acknowledge and affirm His right to claim that scroll.

**⁵ "But one of the elders said to me, 'Stop weeping!
See! The Lion who sprang from the tribe of Judah, who
belongs to the line of David, has conquered, so that He can
open the book and break its seven seals.' ⁶ Then I saw,
midway between the throne and the four living creatures,
standing among the elders, a Lamb that looked as though
He had been slaughtered. He had seven horns and seven
eyes; the latter are the seven spirits of God which are sent
on duty to every portion of the earth."**

(Williams) Revelation 5:5, 6

This is an odd image, but remember it is a coded message, part of which has been given to us. The eyes represent
the God's Holy Spirit. The horns represent Christ's strength.

The message: Jesus' death *looked* to be the end and a
terrific failure, but He had the strength and the wisdom that
comes from seeing things through the eyes of God. He had
God's perspective on life. That perspective brings with it the
strength in every facet of life on earth that had suffered corruption from our Creator's original design and intent.

Now Let's See What Happens

**⁷ "He came and took the book from the right hand
of Him who was seated on the throne.**

[8] When He took it, the four living creatures and the twenty-four elders fell down before the Lamb, each with a harp, and golden bowls that were full of incense, which represent the prayers of God's people.

[9] Then they sang a new song: "You deserve to take the book and break its seals, because you have been slaughtered, and with your blood have bought men from every tribe, tongue, people, and nation,

[10] and have made them a kingdom of priests for our God; and they will rule over the earth."

[11] Then I looked and heard the voices of many angels surrounding the throne, the living creatures, and the elders. Their number was myriads of myriads and thousands of thousands,

[12] saying in a loud voice: "The Lamb that was slaughtered deserves to receive power, riches, wisdom, might, honor, glory, and blessing."

[13] Then I heard every creature in heaven, on earth, underneath the earth, and on the sea, and all that they contain, say: "Blessing, honor, glory, and power be to Him who is seated on the throne and to the Lamb forever."

[14] Then the four living creatures said, "Amen!" And the elders fell down and worshiped."

(Williams) Revelation 5: 7-14

Those horns deserve to be crowned with power, riches, wisdom, might, honor, glory and blessing.

This is the Coronation of Jesus Christ, Lord of Heaven and Earth. The Cross changed everything.

Remember that scene from the movie, *Ever After*, when the hateful woman and her daughter were summoned to the royal court, unaware that the Prince had married the despised Danielle? At that moment their world changed. They were stripped of their position, title and authority. Keep that idea in your mind and let's move on.

WHO IS MISSING?

Missing from the proceedings are the signatories—those witnesses who had been present at the origination of this document—able to verify and validate its contents by pressing their mark into the seals.

Armed with this information, Revelation Chapter Six takes on an entirely different meaning than current interpretations have led many to believe. Chapter Six is John's record of the summoning of signatories: the four described as horse riders. Why? In ancient days, horses were the fastest mode of transportation. The riders of horses carried announcements, messages and legal proclamations that had to go to the boundaries of a kingdom in the swiftest way possible.[60]

SIGNATORIES AND THEIR SEALS

Jesus is placed in authority (power) over every area of earth.

SIGNATORY NUMBER ONE IS SUMMONED

[1] **"Then I saw when the Lamb broke one of the seven seals, and I heard one of the four living creatures saying as with a voice of thunder, "Come[61]." [2] I looked, and behold, a white horse, and he who sat on it had a bow; and a crown was given to him, and he went out conquering and to conquer."**

(NASB) Revelation 6:1, 2

Who is this bow-wielding being who had been given a crown with an appetite for power? The answer is found by looking back in history. Genesis 1 says that God created humanity and put them in a position of authority. In Genesis 3 we learn that Adam and Eve rejected God's plans in favor of the sense-appeal plan that proved contrary to the ways of God. When we became a conquered people the crown (authority) was surrendered. Signatory Number One who fixed his seal as a witness to that treasonous act was Satan. Seal Number One refers to man's relationship with Satan.

SIGNATORY NUMBER TWO SUMMONED

³ **"When He broke the second seal, I heard the second living creature saying, "Come"** ⁴ **And another, a red horse, went out; and to him who sat on it, it was granted to take peace from the earth, and that men would slay one another; and a great sword was given to him."**

(NASB) Revelation 6:3, 4

Again, there are questions to be answered. Who is this? Who gave him the sword and the authority to take peace from the earth, resulting in humans murdering one another?

Remember the symbolism established in previous chapters. Jesus uses a sword, yes. That sword is words of truth. So the 'great sword' this messenger/signatory uses would also be words. However, his words are contrary to truth. They are lies, which foster jealousy, hate and murder. When did that horrific reality come into being? When fear became humanity's motivator, and self-preservation became the objective.

In Genesis 3:9-12 we read how Adam attempted to impose all the blame on Eve, in an effort to absolve himself of any responsibility or guilt.[62] This mind-set, in very short order, produces murder. In Genesis Chapter 4 we read the account of Abel's murder at the hand of his brother, Cain.

This signatory-witness to the ushering in of hate, lies, conflict and murder affixed his mark to the document as witness Number Two. Fear, hate and murder became a part of human relationships. Seal Number Two refers to man's relationship to man.

SIGNATORY NUMBER THREE

[5] "**When He broke the third seal, I heard the third living creature saying, "Come". I looked, and behold, a black horse; and he who sat on it had a pair of scales in his hand.** [6] **And I heard something like a voice in the center of the four living creatures saying, "A quart of wheat for a denarius, and three quarts of barley for a denarius; and do not damage the oil and the wine."**

(NASB) Revelation 6:5, 6

To set the stage for this universal reality, again we will go back to the beginning. Genesis 2:1-25 tells about the forming of Adam. Verse 5 says something interesting: there was not a man to till the ground. Through Adam, God introduced the cultivation of crops. Man working with the earth.

Now read Genesis 3:17-19. As a direct result of the choice man made to establish an existence rooted in principals contrary to the life and love of God. The earth itself became cursed.

Scales have the same symbolic meaning to the ancients as they do to us: justice. Genesis Chapters 6 through 8 describe the execution of the Heavenly Court's decision made 3,000 years prior to the proceedings John is involved with in Revelation.

Look specifically at Genesis 6:17; 7:21-23; and 8:15-22. All air-breathing beings—except those in the ark—died in the flood. Plant life would survive.

Cultivating crops became the means of survival, which elevated their value tremendously. Now look at God's declaration of Genesis 8:22.

"While the earth *remains, seedtime and harvest, cold and heat, winter and summer, and day and night shall not cease."*

Genesis 8:22

The earth was completely changed as a result of the flood. The pre-flood terrarium environment was destroyed forever, giving us the earth as we know it today: with seasons, unprotected exposure to the sun's rays, violent swings in temperature and unpredictable weather patterns.

Humanity's survival would depend on their ability to grow and preserve crops. Jump forward to the introduction of the Law in Deuteronomy, and we find God instructing the people to include barley, wheat, oil and wine in their worship, and a means by which they would be blessed by Him. Deuteronomy 11:1-32

"I will give you rain for your land in season, the early rain and the late rain, that you may gather in your grain, your wine and your oil."

Deuteronomy 11:14

Grain, wine and oil are included in the passage from Deuteronomy, which the Israelites were commanded to recite morning and evening and to write upon the doorposts of their houses and upon the gates of their cities:

"If you pay heed to the commandments I give you this day... And I will provide pasture in your fields for your cattle; and you shall eat your fill. Take heed lest you be lured away

131

and turn aside to serve other gods and worship them, and the anger of the Lord be kindled against you, and He shut up the heavens, so that there will be no rain, and the land not yield its harvest...."

Deuteronomy 11:13-16

The third signatory's mark affixed to the sealed document is justice. It deals with man's relationship with the earth.

FOURTH SIGNATORY

[7]And when he had opened the fourth seal, I heard the voice of the fourth beast say, Come and see. [8]And I looked, and behold a pale horse: and his name that sat on him was Death, and Hell followed with him. And power was given unto them over the fourth part of the earth, to kill with sword, and with hunger, and with death, and with the beasts of the earth."

NASB Revelation 6: 7, 8

The worldwide ramifications of the previous three seals culminates in the fourth. Had mankind chosen God's ways, life would have been the outcome. However, by choosing the enemy's ways, death resulted. This standard tainted everything on earth, not only humans. The animal kingdom, down to the microbial level was forever altered, as well. What had been created as a habitat perfectly suited became hostile and dangerous. Enemies abounded. The fourth seal refers to man's relationship with the animal kingdom.

Historically, these four witnesses cover the time beginning with the fall in the Garden until the Father was able to find a man, who was willing to enter into a covenant partnership.[63] He needed a man who would commit himself and his future generations to seeing God's promise of salvation and redemption. God found Abram. Because Abram entered into that covenant with God, human history changed course once again. John continues to watch the legal proceedings. He's seen the effects of the fall on the history of humanity.

Seal Number Five

[9] When He broke the fifth seal, I saw underneath the altar the souls of those who had been slaughtered for being faithful to God's message and for the testimony they bore to it.

[10] Then in a loud voice they cried out, "Holy and true Master, how long will you refrain from charging and avenging our blood upon the inhabitants of the earth?"

[11] Then a white robe was given to each of them, and they were told to keep quiet a little while longer, until the

number of their fellow-slaves and brothers, who were killed as they had been, was complete."

(Williams) Revelation 6:9-11

You will notice the opening of the fifth seal does not include a summons. Why? Because the One securing His seal to this moment in history is already present.

This deals with the Covenant of Redemption initiated by the Lord God Jehovah through Abram, expanded upon and clarified through Moses by the laws God gave concerning righteousness[64] (the way it was meant to be).

The former covenant was intended to be an interim system, a stopgap measure used only until the final solution was implemented. The stopgap, in this case, is the atoning of sin through animal sacrifice.[65]

What John records here is the 2,000 years of substitutionary animal sacrifice. This idea is a radical departure from what has become the accepted interpretation of this passage, but let's take a deeper look.

What kind of meaning and implication would the phrase "Under the altar" hold for the first-century Hebrew reader[66]?

With only one legitimate altar that could be used in the worship of God and for the purpose of temporarily atoning sin, which is found in only one place on the planet, the message is very clear. The altar John speaks of could only point in one direction; the covenant of promise which required animal sacrifices. A system that was "a shadow of what now is the Body of Christ.[67]" Located in the Temple in the city of Jerusalem.

The word John used in describing those beings under the laws of altar sacrifice is the word *psuche*, the Greek equivalent of the Hebrew word, *nephesh*.

The definition: that which is manifested in animals, animal life; hence, breath (not breath as mere air, but as the sign of life).[68]

The word 'souls' is not exclusively used in reference to human beings. In fact, John's use of it reinforces the idea that they are the animals whose blood was used in Temple worship. A concept which, at first blush, might be hard to consider. However, when coupled with the word's of Jesus that tells us The Father knows when a sparrow falls, to think these creatures slaughtered for the purpose of atoning for the sins of man are not cast aside and unrewarded, suddenly seems less far-fetched.

What kind of souls were slaughtered (sacrificed) during that 2,000 year period between God's promise to Abraham and Christ's fulfillment of that promise? Animals. What witness or testimony did they hold?

Let's look at the ritual in which each of these sacrificed animals participated once deemed and judged to be a worthy sacrifice. The priests would lay hands upon the heads of the animals and speak the sins of the people over them, transferring the human's guilt and prescribed punishment onto the substitute. When the animal was slain, the human who had committed the sins was to say, "It should have been me."

The testimony they held was the sin of the human for which they were killed and the promise that the day was coming when God's plan would be fulfilled; man would be redeemed from the curse of the law. These slaughtered sacrifices had some questions: When is our blood and the lives we gave in honor and worship to the Word of God going to be avenged? How much longer is this going to go on[69]?

The answer: Just a little while longer, there is a quota that is not yet satisfied.[70] When that is met, you will witness the fulfillment. Your blood will no longer be used to hold the sins of humanity. However, until that day, these holders of guilt and sin are given a righteous covering enabling them to remain in the presence of Holiness, in spite of the guilt they have been commissioned to carry.

The fifth seal covers the time from Abraham to Christ and deals with man's relationship with God under the former covenant. The Hebrew meaning of the number corresponding to this seal is: look, reveal and breath[71].

Seal Number Six

For the modern-day reader, the person who has wondered why Revelation was even included in the Bible, the answer to that question is found in John's recording of what happened with seal Number 6.

[12] When He broke the sixth seal, I looked, and there was a great earthquake, and the sun turned black as sackcloth, and the full moon became like blood, [13] and the stars of the sky fell to the earth, just as a fig tree, when shaken by a violent wind, drops its unripe figs. [14] The sky

was swept away just like a scroll that is rolled up; and every mountain and island was moved out of its place. [15]The kings of the earth, the great men, the military leaders, the rich, the mighty—everybody, whether slaves or free—hid themselves in the caves and among the rocks of the mountains. [16]And they said to the mountains and the rocks: "Fall on us and conceal us from the sight of Him who is seated on the throne, and from the anger of the Lamb, [17]because the great day of their anger has come, and who can stand it?"

(Williams) Revelation 6:12-17

Reading this from a modern-day, purely literal perspective makes this passage appear terrifying. Remember this is a message buried in symbolism and meant to be unearthed. When its hidden meaning is discovered the reader will, as promised, find themselves blessed, empowered and happy.

Often the more frightening the image, the greater the treasure it is attempting to protect.

What is John's message? To find out, we are going to have to decode it using ancient, Biblical symbolism.

First, we have an earthquake.

Symbolically, an earthquake speaks of dethroning governing powers. Matthew tells us that there was an earth-

138

quake at the time of the crucifixion.[72] This is exactly what happened when the Lord ratified the Covenant of Redemption on the Cross. The former governing power that had reigned over every man, woman and child on the planet was stripped of its authority to rule the hearts and lives of humanity.[73]

Secondly, the sun is darkened.

Three gospel accounts report the sun was darkened when Christ was on the Cross.[74] With two of these things having occurred on the physical plane, it is easy to surmise that Heaven is announcing to the world what is taking place on the universal, eternal, spiritual plane. Certainly an interpretation worthy of serious consideration if one professes to believe that the Cross had an impact on history.

Next consider symbolic meanings associated with the sun, moon, stars, fig trees and unripened fruit.

The first time we read of the sun, moon and stars referenced together is in Genesis 37. Joseph[75] dreamed a dream in which the sun, moon and eleven stars bowed down to him. The meaning, symbolized by those celestial bodies, was apparent to his family members. It is the nation of Israel and that first generation, who did not appreciate the dream's message.

A word about trees. "When we think of a tree an image comes to mind, but when the Hebrews, who wrote the Bible, think of a tree an action comes to mind. This is one of the foundational differences between Ancient Hebrew and modern Western thought. The Hebrew word *eyts* represents a tree, but more the action of lifting up with support, the function of the trunk and branches of the tree."[76]

Fig trees symbolize Israel's national privilege.[77] Being aware of this explains the anger unleashed on Jesus in Matthew 26:3-4 after He cursed the fig tree in Matthew 21:19-21. The religious leaders knew the inferred meaning behind His actions and the words He spoke concerning the tree, *"Let no fruit grow on thee henceforward forever."*

You will remember, from previous chapters, that mountains are symbolic of prideful governing authorities both legitimate and illegitimate.

Sky rolled back as a scroll. Similar to an ancient Hebrew idiom which means to return to a previous state or place.[78] The image is of the sun rolling back in preparation to again rise.

Now let's read what Jesus had to say about sun, moon, stars and seated powers when He spoke of the Temple's destruction and the fall of Jerusalem.

> *"Immediately after the tribulation of those days shall the sun be darkened, and the moon shall not give her light, and the stars shall fall from heaven, and the powers of the heavens shall be shaken..."*
>
> Matthew 24:29

Sounds like John is quoting, verbatim, what he heard the Lord say when they were together that **day** just before the crucifixion, doesn't it?

When Jesus succeeded in His mission to redeem man from the mess we had gotten ourselves into and return us to the presence of the Father, everything was turned rightside-up. What is the hidden message of Revelation 6:12-17? Here is what it looks like when we plug in the literal meanings for the symbolic images:

When Jesus removed the sixth seal I saw a massive shift in the foundation of the earth. Israel, the nation with whom God joined in covenant; and had been entrusted

141

with His authentic word with which they were to bring light to the world, reflect His glory and teach His ways no longer holds that position.

Why? Because Jesus Christ has fulfilled the requirements of that first covenant.

This new and better covenant so far exceeds the former! Not only does it shake the very foundation upon which the earth is seated, changing the present and future, it is powerful enough and intended to roll back—reset if you will—to the way things were intended to be at the beginning.

Every governing authority both large and small, which was established and operates under the old regime, is stripped of its authority. Those ways are no longer legitimate, being outside of the authority of Christ.

All who cling desperately to the positions, stations authority and standards they held under the former ways are in trouble. Attempting to maintain things the way it ran under the former rule, as if nothing changed, is foolishness!

Whether those positions were of kings, slaves, rich, poor, powerful or downtrodden is irrelevant. The previous regime has been ousted; but many will try to hide within the former ways and behind the remnants of the old system. They will attempt to do so because they do not want to serve the new King. Why? Because they believe God is angry and Jesus is fed-up and that they are not forgiven, accepted or loved by the Father. This is not true. We know differently and it is our responsibility to pro-

claim the truth. There is peace between God and man because Jesus has fulfilled the enemy's ransom demands.

(Author's Paraphrase) Revelation 6:12-17

At this point there are more questions to be asked:

- Do I believe that the Cross of Christ was far-reaching enough to accomplish all that the removal of the sixth seal reveals?
- Am I guilty of clinging to the status quo imposed by the old regime?
- Do I believe that the Kingdom of God's ways are completely contrary to the kingdom of this world's ways?
- What kingdom do I operate in?
- Which King do I serve?

The sixth seal began at the Cross and will remain throughout eternity. It is the Covenant made between the Father and Jesus, which reestablishes man's ability to be in relationship with God.

12

Emancipation!

Salvation has come! The Sixth Seal, accomplished by Our Lord Jesus Christ on the Cross, has indeed changed everything. John records what happened as a result of Christ's self-sacrifice.

CHANGE IS IN THE AIR

¹And after these things I saw four angels standing on the four corners of the earth, holding the four winds of the earth, that the wind should not blow on the earth, nor on the sea, nor on any tree."

Revelation Chapter 7:1

After what things? All that took place in the earth as a result of the Cross! The old regime—lorded over by the enemy and held in place by the guilt of humanity—has been rendered powerless because of Christ and all He accomplished. He exchanged His righteousness for our sin! In so doing, He satisfied the demands of the law of sin and death—the horrible system humanity adopted at the Fall in the garden. That was the foundation of the world's system, which is why, at the foundation of the world's system of government, (not the creation of the universe) we are told that Christ was slain.[79] At the moment man chose to follow that direction, the only way out of that world's system was for a man to overcome the world's system.

Now John sees the prison wardens. The beings charged with keeping the earth, humanity (seas) in general and teaching/ministry (trees) in particular, deprived of spiritual Truth (wind); separating us from the very Life of God. Similar imagery is used in Genesis 3:24 describing what happened at the Garden.

[2] "And I saw another angel ascending from the East, having the seal of the living God: and he cried with a loud voice to the four angels, to whom it was given to hurt the earth and the sea,[3] Saying, Hurt not the earth, neither the sea, nor the trees, till we have sealed the servants of our God in their foreheads."[80] [4] And I heard the number of them which were sealed: and there were sealed an hundred

and forty and four thousand of all the tribes of the children of Israel. ⁵ Of the tribe of Juda were sealed twelve thousand. Of the tribe of Reuben were sealed twelve thousand. Of the tribe of Gad were sealed twelve thousand. ⁶ Of the tribe of Aser were sealed twelve thousand. Of the tribe of Nephthalim were sealed twelve thousand. Of the tribe of Manasses were sealed twelve thousand. ⁷ Of the tribe of Simeon were sealed twelve thousand. Of the tribe of Levi were sealed twelve thousand. Of the tribe of Issachar were sealed twelve thousand. ⁸ Of the tribe of Zabulon were sealed twelve thousand. Of the tribe of Joseph were sealed twelve thousand. Of the tribe of Benjamin were sealed twelve thousand.

Revelation 7:2-8

Another angel (of a different kind) rises from the East. The word east has a greater meaning to the ancients than a simple compass point. East speaks of the beginning, the dawn, the origin. And didn't John just describe seeing history rolled back like a scroll? Our modern-day term would be retroactive. This angel has a new message. A message that comes from the future, because it took 4,000 years to secure, but God is making this law retroactive. Hard to believe? Perhaps at first, but our hypothesis says, "The Cross changed everything." That includes history.

147

This messenger carries the seal of the Living God and is commissioned to find and mark for God those who have dedicated their lives in service to Him. John records the number of dedicated servants found, whose lives were devoted to honoring The One True Living God: 12,000 from each of the 12 tribes of Israel. This means, that from the moment God and Abraham entered into that covenant and Abraham granted the Lord God Jehovah access to humanity through his lineage, and Jesus' final act of sacrifice, there were found 144,000 human beings that faithfully served God.

And Abraham called the name of that place Jehovah jireh: as it is said to this day, In the mount of the LORD it shall be seen. [15] And the angel of the Lord called unto Abraham out of heaven the second time, [16] And said, By myself have sworn, saith the LORD, for because thou hast done this thing, and hast not withheld thy son, thine only son:

[17] That in blessing I will bless thee, and in multiplying I will multiply thy seed as the stars of the heaven, and as the sand which is upon the sea shore; and thy seed shall possess the gate of his enemies; [18] And in thy seed shall all the nations of the earth be blessed; because thou hast obeyed my voice."

Genesis 22:14-18

In thy seed (Jesus) shall all of the nations of the earth be blessed. This is absolutely true. So what significance does the 12,000 of every tribe hold?

That, I believe, is found in Deuteronomy.

⁸ "When the Most High divided to the nations their inheritance, when he separated the sons of Adam, he set the bounds of the people according to the number of the children of Israel. ⁹ For the LORD's portion is his people; Jacob is the lot of his inheritance."

Deuteronomy 32:8-9

Through the nation of Israel, all people would be blessed. Israel would represent all of humanity and satisfy the legal requirements set forth in the laws of sin and death. Remember the Lord's answer to the question asked by the souls under the altar: "When the number of your fellow-servants is complete."

Then we immediately see the people of the nation of Israel numbered and can easily surmise that the number needed to fulfill the requirement is 12,000 from each tribe. Why? Again we look to the meaning of numbers in the Hebrew tradition. 1,000 means complete, over and above. Far exceeding. The number 12 means perfected government. So the meaning, from a Hebrew perspective, is the Lord God Jehovah satisfied the demands of our ransom because there were 144,000 human beings in whom His government was perfected, people who faithfully and loyally served only Him. They did not ever turn away and serve other gods[81].

When that number was confirmed, John saw something truly amazing:

> [9] "**After this I beheld, and, lo, a great multitude, which no man could number, of all nations, and kindreds, and people, and tongues, stood before the throne, and before the Lamb, clothed with white robes, and palms in their hands;**
> [10] **And cried with a loud voice, saying, Salvation to our God which sitteth upon the throne, and unto the Lamb.**
> [11] **And all the angels stood round about the throne, and about the elders and the four beasts, and fell before the throne on their faces, and worshipped God,**
> [12] **Saying, Amen: Blessing, and glory, and wisdom, and thanksgiving, and honour, and power, and might, be unto our God forever and ever. Amen"**

Revelation 7:9-12

What a magnificent sight! What a glorious plan! And every being surrounding the throne are beside themselves watching this plan unfold before their eyes! Worthy of worship? Oh yes!

Humanity has been released from the death sentence! Not only the nation of Israel, but just as God had promised,

"All the nations of the earth are blessed, because Abraham trusted God." Wow!

One of the elders asked John if he knew who these people were and where they came from.

¹³ "**And one of the elders answered, saying unto me, What are these which are arrayed in white robes? and whence came they?**

John said to the Elder, "You know, how about you tell me."

¹⁴ **And I said unto him, Sir, thou knowest. And he said to me, These are they which came out of great tribulation, and have washed their robes, and made them white in the blood of the Lamb.**

¹⁵ **Therefore are they before the throne of God, and serve him day and night in his temple: and he that sitteth on the throne shall dwell among them.**

¹⁶ **They shall hunger no more, neither thirst anymore; neither shall the sun light on them, nor any heat.**

¹⁷ **For the Lamb which is in the midst of the throne shall feed them, and shall lead them unto living fountains of waters: and God shall wipe away all tears from their eyes."**

Revelation 7: 13-17

The Cross changed everything! Salvation was extended beyond the confines of the nation of Israel. The Lord's righteousness is extended to all who trust in Him for their salvation.

13

John's Warning Begins

John has witnessed the most earthshaking moment in history. The host of humanity has been released from the bondage of sin and death, and freedom of choice has been restored. Why is that different? What has changed? Fundamentally everything!

Paul, in the Book of Romans, does a phenomenal job of explaining the differences between existing under the old regime and living life in the new. See the short answer in the Book of Romans.

For if by one man's offense death reigned through that one, to a much greater degree will those who continue to receive the overflow of His unmerited favor and His gift of right standing with Himself, reign in real life through One, Jesus Christ.

[18]*"So, as through one offense there resulted condemnation for all men, just so through one act of uprightness there resulted right standing involving life for all men.*
[19]*For just as by that man's disobedience the whole race of men were constituted sinners, so by this One's obedience the whole race of men may be brought into right standing with God."*

(Williams) Romans 5:18-19

Adam set the course for all who followed after him; a standard that attempted to make men right. That standard was nothing more than a sliding scale set by the individual based on what they viewed as right and wrong, good and evil. Watch any three-year-old, and you see this principle at work. It needs to be my way! That is what it means to become like god, knowing (or believing we know) by the information we are able to take in through our physical senses, how to determine what is right and what is wrong. Every decision hinged on how it affects me and securely anchored in my opinion. Multiply that by every person born on this planet, and the miracle is we haven't completely annihilated the human race.

What happens when you do something that I have deemed as evil? You've stolen my parking spot or cut me off in traffic or hurt my feelings or have what I want or refuse to play by the rules that I have established in my mind for the way things are supposed to be. I demand you play by my rules, or I hurt you. Things like road rage becomes justified in our own minds. Shunning, gossip, hate, murder and thoughts that say, "They got what they deserved," and "you'll pay for that," are all remnants of the Adam way of life. Was that God's plan?

No!

That's the plan we established and continue, for the most part, to maintain. Why? Because it makes sense to us. It appeals to our human senses. Remember in Genesis, Adam weighed his decision based on what made sense to his physical senses when choosing between the structure that would support Life and the structure that supported man making his own judgments regarding what is good and what is bad.

This remains the human challenge. We face decisions daily that require us to look beyond the surface of what we can see, feel, taste, and survey. Will we allow our lives to be

155

governed by the Word of God, or will we go for the, I-don't-think-God-meant- what-He-said defense?

JESUS MODELED THE WAY TEMPTATION IS TO BE HANDLED IN MATTHEW, "IT IS WRITTEN...".

When my kids wanted to stay out past the city curfew or drive past the hour their permits allowed, I used to tell them, "This is not a decision you need to make. It has already been made for you. The law says..." That is essentially the way the Lord handled temptation. He knew what the Law said and that Word was His decision maker.

What does this have to do with the Cross and John's warning? Everything! You see, the problem was, as soon as a human being made a decision in direct opposition to the way of Life, (which is the way this universe was designed to operate) by default, we chose death. Not too bright are we? In choosing death, we chose to live under the rules that governed the kingdom of darkness, and we were subjects of the king, who ruled that kingdom. Once locked in, there was no way out.

Why did the host of heaven fall at the feet of Jesus in worship? Because God had conceived such a magnificent plan, the enemy never saw it coming. Like a movie that keeps you guessing, wondering and off balance. When it ends so surprisingly perfect you sit in silence while the credits roll, replaying the masterpiece in your mind. That is what our Father, our Brother, our King, our Redeemer accomplished on a colossal scale! Jesus, so perfectly executed that plan, that there is nothing for the prosecuting attorney left to accuse us of or argue against. Brilliant—God's plan was absolutely, gloriously brilliant!

Because of the far-reaching effects of the Cross, we are no longer slaves in the kingdom of darkness. We are no longer bound to the laws that govern that kingdom. When the seals were broken—meaning they were removed (forgiven) from us—we were no longer obligated to exist under their demands. We are now free to live our lives empowered and led by the Spirit of God! We have, again, two choices: life or death. God's ways or the enemy's.

THIS IS THE MESSAGE JOHN WAS COMMISSIONED TO RECORD. THIS IS HOW THE CROSS CHANGED EVERYTHING! SO, WHY THE WARNING?

There is a final piece of unfinished business, and it is truly, truly ugly. It is recorded in Matthew.

"Then answered all the people, and said, His blood be on us, and on our children."

Matthew 27:25

For 2,000 years God had maintained the covenant of Abraham, and the nation that began with his son, Isaac. He equated the relationship to that of husband and wife. When the nation strayed from Him and pursued the gods and ways of other nations, He described it as a wife committing adultery.[82]

God is Life, Light and Love. When we refuse Him and reject His ways, we are cutting ourselves off from Life, Light and Love. We find ourselves, just like Adam, crouching behind concepts, hiding behind fruitless leaves and blaming God and everyone else for our condition. Incidentally, wisdom is also a benefit lost when we reject our Creator.

When God extends mercy, He also extends time— time that gives opportunity to repent, to set things right and to transition. That merciful extension ends in Judgment.

The historical timeline we are looking at is between Christ's sacrificial death, burial, and resurrection and when animal sacrifice ended. Historians and eclipse data tell us Christ was most likely crucified at the Passover in 33 AD. The total destruction of the Temple in Jerusalem took place 37 years later in 70 AD.

[1] **"When He broke the seventh seal, there was silence in heaven for about half an hour."**

Revelation 8:1

WHEN THIS ISSUE IS ADDRESSED, ALL OF HEAVEN IS SILENT

For 37 years mercy had been extended, staying the execution of judgment. Those 37 years gave people the opportunity to hear the message of Christ's redemption and make a decision regarding that message and adequate time to transition.

Thirty-seven years is just under the 40 year threshold of the Lord's prophecy concerning the generation that demanded His crucifixion.[83] I propose that the "almost half an hour" silent heaven represents the years of mercy between the sentencing and the execution of that sentence. Our God is mercy-filled. He always warns. He always instructs. He gives time to repent.[84]

Let's set the stage.

Place: Jerusalem

Time: One week before the beginning of Passover through the last day of Second Passover[85] 66AD and The Feast of Pentecost that same year.

Josephus, Jewish historian and eyewitness to the siege of Jerusalem and the destruction of the Temple, writes what happened during the time of Passover 66AD. This can be read in *The Complete Works of Flavius-Josephus*:

> *"Thus there was a star resembling a sword, which stood over the city, and a comet, that continued a whole year. Thus also, before the Jews' rebellion, and before those commotions which preceded the war, when the people were come in great crowds to the feast of unleavened bread, on the eight day of the month Xanthicus, [Nisan,] and at the ninth hour of the night, so great a light shone round the altar and the holy house, that it appeared to be bright day-time; which light lasted for half an hour . This light seemed to be a good sign to the unskillful, but was so interpreted by the sacred scribes as to portend those events that fol- lowed immediately upon it.*
>
> *At the same festival also, a heifer, as she was led by the high priest to be sacrificed, brought forth a lamb in the midst of the temple. Moreover, the Eastern gate of the inner, [court of the temple,] which was of brass, and vastly heavy, and had been with difficulty shut by*

160

twenty men, and rested upon a basis armed with iron, and had bolts fastened very deep into the firm floor, which was there made of one entire stone, was seen to be opened of its own accord about the sixth hour of the night. Now, those that kept watch in the temple came thereupon running to the captain of the temple, and told him of it; who then came up thither, and not without great difficulty was able to shut the gate again. This also appeared to the vulgar to be a very happy prodigy, as if God did thereby open them the gate of happiness. But the men of learning understood it, that the security of their holy house was dissolved of its own accord, and that the gate was opened for the advantage of their enemies. So these publicly declared, that this signal forshewed the desolation that was coming upon them.

Besides these, a few days after that feast, on the one-and-twentieth day of the month Artemisius, [Jyar,] a certain prodigious and incredible phenomenon appeared; I suppose the account of it would seem to be a fable, were it not related by those that saw it, and were not the events that followed it of so considerable a nature as to deserve such signals; for, before sun-setting, chariots and troops of soldiers in their armour were seen running about among the clouds, and surrounding of cities. Moreover, at that feast which we call Pentecost, as the priests were going by night into the inner [court of the] temple, as their custom was, to perform their sacred ministrations, they said that, in the first place, they felt a quaking, and heard a great

161

noise, and after that they heard a sound as of a great multitude, saying, "Let us remove hence." [86]

The stage is set. When John witnesses the Lord remove the final seal, John watches the unfolding of events that have yet to take place on earth. Seeing the soon-to-be execution of the judgment against Jerusalem and the generation who declared, "His blood be on us and on our children," fueled the urgency with which he dispersed this warning.

²Then I saw the seven angels who stand before God, and seven trumpets were given to them.
³ Then another angel with a sensor of gold came and stood at the altar, and a great quantity of incense was given to him to mingle with the prayers of all God's people, on the altar of gold that stood before the throne.
⁴So the smoke of the incense went up from the angel's hand to the presence of God for the prayers of His people: ⁵Then the angel took the censer, filled it with fire from the altar, and flung it to the earth, and there followed peals of thunder with its rumblings, flashes of lightning, and an earthquake.
⁶And the seven angels with the seven trumpets prepared to blow them.

(Williams) Revelation 8:2-6

It is hard to refute how seamlessly the prophetic warning describes the events reported by historians to have occurred in Jerusalem between the time of Passover (spring of 66 AD) and three and a half years later in August of 70AD.

The events leading to the fall of Jerusalem in 70AD at the hands of the Roman army—led by Titus—are well documented. The civil unrest, the political conflict, economic disparity, religious/spiritual imposition and impropriety converged into the perfect storm. Anyone interested in delving more deeply into the specifics of those events will find a plethora of information to digest.[87] We will just try to hit the bullet points.

14

Groundwork Is Laid

When the silence ended, the messengers' trumpets blew, announcing the execution of the judgment. The fallout of that judgment would affect all who were in Jerusalem; those who had resolutely rejected God's plan and continued in the former tradition. Those who did not heed the warnings given decades earlier by Christ[88] or this warning by John, or those who might just happen to be there on business. Whatever the reason for them being in the city would soon prove irrelevant. The deluge would be without discrimination.

Things were coming apart on every side. Rome had appointed men to hold the position of High Priest.[89] They disregarded God's instruction and qualification guidelines for men holding that powerful political/religious/civil position.

165

The Fox Was in Charge of the Hen House

Other sources reveal that Yeshua (Jason) offered Antiochus an exorbitant bribe to appoint him high priest. After having served in this post for some time, Menelaus (according to this source not a brother of Yeshua, nor even a kohen of the priestly family) promised the king an even greater sum, and was promptly given the post. Both these nominees had promised the king their utmost cooperation to enforce the king's pet project of Hellenizing the country, by forcibly spreading Greek culture…

…The High Priest ruled over the temple. He was appointed by Herod for the duration he desired, and often won his office through treachery or bribery. Beginning with the Maccabean revolt and up until the time of Herod-the high priest was the leading religious and political figure in Jerusalem.

After Herod's death and the removal of Archelaus, the appointing of the high priest passed to the Roman governors of Jerusalem."[90]

The death of James, the brother of Jesus Christ and leader of the church at Jerusalem is murdered in 62AD[91].

This event surely announced to all Christ Followers that Jerusalem was too dangerous and hostile an environment in which to remain.

Greed and corruption are rampant, Rome's Ceasars are exalted and extolled as gods, complete with worship and sacrificial demands made on the people under their control.

- 64AD The Great Fire destroyed 75% of the city of Rome. The populace accused Nero. Nero, in turn laid the blame and guilt on the Christians, whom he had killed in the most horrific of ways. His reign of terror ended with his suicide four years later.

- 65AD Gennius Florus is appointed by Rome as Governor of Judea. His five-year reign marked with greed and unparalleled cruelty and injustice.[92]

- 66AD was filled with strange and ominous happenings during the festivals held in Jerusalem that year.

On a single spring day-Iyar 16, 66AD 3,600 Jewish citizens of Jerusalem are slaughtered at the command of Florus. This marks the beginning of the Jewish revolt against Rome.

The next three and a half years are horrific for anyone remaining in the city,[93] and can be separated into three distinct divisions: the revolt, civil war, siege/destruction.

John is writing this document in this political climate. The need for this message to be communicated is undeniable, but it is very dangerous to speak against the Roman government, Roman Caesars, Rome's appointed governors, leaders and High Priests. His readers are not living in Jerusalem or in Judea at the time, but that is where they are from. It is their home country, and they have ties there and quite possibly loved ones as well. This warning must get out!

[7] **"The first one blew his trumpet, and there was a shower of hail and fire mixed with blood as it hurled itself upon the earth, and one-third of the earth was burned up, and all the green grass was burned up.**
[8]Then the second angel blew his trumpet, and what seemed to be a great mountain all ablaze with fire hurled itself into the sea, and one-third of the sea was turned into blood,
[9]and one-third of all the living creatures in the sea perished, and one-third of the ships were destroyed.
[10]Then the third angel blew his trumpet, and there fell from the sky a great star blazing like a torch, and it fell upon one-third of the rivers and the springs of water.

¹¹The star is called Absinthus, that is, Wormwood. So one-third of the waters turned to wormwood, and great numbers of people died of the waters, because they had turned bitter."

(Williams) Revelation 8:7-11

Let's look at this symbolically. We will use metaphoric definitions already established and explore possibilities for those being introduced and see if these passages of scripture might point to any literal fulfillment. We'll keep in mind that what is lost to us was clearly evident to John's Jewish audience, exactly as designed.

We will begin by exploring the meaning(s) connected to the number *3*. Three refers to unity[94].

> *"One symbolizes unity, agreement, simplicity. When something exists alone, nothing disturbs it. It remains completely at peace, without regard for anything else.*
> *Two symbolizes duality, tension and complexity.*
> *The number three symbolizes a harmony that includes and synthesizes two opposites. The unity symbolized by the number three isn't accomplished by getting rid of number two, the entity that caused the discord, and reverting to the unity symbolized by number one. Rather, three merges the two to create a new entity, one that harmoniously includes both opposites."*

When a third part of the harmonizing factor is removed, all that is left exists in discord and conflict. John's multiple reference of thirds being removed speaks of irreconcilable conflict.

Hail mixed with blood destroys one-third of the land and all green grass. In Isaiah 37, God speaks to the people living in Jerusalem 700 years earlier facing the terrors of siege and conquest. The inhabitants of this region (Judea) and its seat of power (Jerusalem) back then were referred to as green grass,[95] plants and herbs, being destroyed before reaching maturity or fruitful age.

Blood and hail were the first and seventh of the Egyptian plagues, brought upon them for disobedience and refusing to honor the commands of God. John's warning: all is in discord when the harmonizing factor is removed. Choosing to remain in that environment will ensure that your life and purpose will not reach a mature/fruitful end.

The second trumpet blast announced the arrival of what "seemed to be a great blazing mountain hurl itself into the sea, which turned one-third of the sea to blood and caused one-third of all creatures living in the sea to die and one-third of the sea vessels to be destroyed.

Remember, mountains represent governing authorities (either legitimate or illegitimate) and pride. You'll recall that sea represents humanity, and it also represents the place where mountains are brought down to equal level, no longer exalted above sea level.

John tells of a prideful, governing authority hurling itself into the midst of an earthly human population. This would be an illegitimate, but powerful authority. This hot-shot, power-wielding, pride-filled entity sets itself up as ruling dictator, and in so doing, the harmonizing factor is removed. Only conflict remains.

God created humans to harmonize in three parts: body, soul and spirit. Going back to the garden, what do we see? The warning of death connected with the fruit of the knowledge of good/evil did not immediately strike Adam and Eve's physical bodies, did it? No. What died in them was their connection to Life. They could no longer connect or communicate with the Source of Life, Light and Love. Their souls existed in darkness, and their bodies eventually died.

171

This second trumpet warns that the same danger holds true. Lives will be lost on all three levels: body, soul and spirit. No one will be spared because the harmonizing factor on every level will be attacked.

The vessels described as ships are the bodies we must have to operate on the earth. Human bodies are the vessels that carry the Love of God, the message of the Kingdom and the power of the Holy Spirit. When faced with this mountain that crashes into their midst, the vessels (individuals) of the sea (humanity) will be relieved of the part that makes for unity.

The third trumpet warns of a great blazing star falling like a torch upon the fresh water sources. It pollutes the waters, causing them to become bitter. When the people consume this bitter water, it kills them.

Water is truth and life. John,[96] in his gospel tells us that Jesus described himself as being Living water. To drink the waters of His teaching would bring life, what does it mean that all the drinkable water supplies are made bitter by a star (remember stars are messengers) and result in death for those who drink of them? This messenger/angel has been hurled out of the presence of God and perverts the water supply (the word of God). More conflict. More discord. More death.

This holds true today. When we submit to teachers whose teachings pollute Truth, we can recognize the poison because we become bitter, and our lives no longer produce what God's Spirit desires: love, joy, peace, patience, temperance, kindness, goodness, faithfulness, and gentleness.

Take a quick inventory of your beliefs—beliefs about yourself, others and God. Do those beliefs produce bitterness, discord and things contrary to Spirit of God? If so, you have a mountain in your midst that is not a legitimate authority in your life, and it needs to be removed!

15

Jerusalem Implodes

¹² "Then the fourth angel blew his trumpet, and one-third of the sun was cursed with a plague, and one-third of the moon, and one-third of the stars, so that one-third of them were darkened, and there was no light for one-third of the day and for one-third of the night."

Revelation 8:12

The conflict continues. Here again is the sun, moon and stars, and we will be keeping with the earlier reference from Joseph's dream that these indicate the nation of Israel. The nation is plagued with a curse limiting the ability to do their job—bring light to the world. Why? Conflict and discord.

Looking to historian's accounts of the three and a half years preceding the total destruction of the Temple at Jerusalem in 70AD, we learn that the ancient city divided into three political and ideological groups, which became three civil-warring factions responsible for much of the horror experienced within the walls of the city.

****¹³ **"Then I looked, and I heard an eagle flying in mid-air say in a loud voice, "Alas! Alas! Alas for the inhabitants of the earth because of the remaining blasts of the three angels who are going to blow their trumpets!"**

Revelation 8:13

Rome (whose symbol was the eagle) sets their sights on destroying the Jewish people and conquering the city of Jerusalem. These three remaining trumpet blasts are played out in and around Jerusalem during what Jesus described as a time of great tribulation.[97] This time of great tribulation is divided into three phases:

- The Great Revolt (which lasted three and a half months)
- The Great Civil War (which continued sporadically throughout the entire three and a half years)

- The Great Siege (lasting five months and resulting in the fall of Jerusalem and the total destruction of the Temple).

Phase One: The Great Revolt

The revolt, which began in August of 66, was initially viewed as a victory. After seven days of bloody battle the Romans retreated. Many of the Jews took this to be a sign that God was going to use their nation to conquer and defeat Rome once and for all and restore them to their former glory. (We will call these folks the Rebel Zealots.) Others in the city disagreed. Vehemently. (We will call them the Peace-Seeking Moderates.) These two factions along with the Religious Leaders made up the first three-way split of the city.

Phase Two: The Great Civil War

These three factions turned on one another, which sparked the beginning of a civil war. While the people in Jerusalem fought and killed one another, "ethnic cleansing" began in the Judean villages. Greeks were killing Jews by the thousands. And Rome sent their 12th Legion- stationed to the north in Syria down through Galilee and Judea to Jerusalem.

In Jerusalem, the first faction to be completely wiped out was the Religious Leaders. That void was soon replaced by a militia group, led by John of Gischala. This group represented the villagers, whose pleas for assistance had been ignored by the Jewish leaders in Jerusalem, who had refused to send help. Seems they were too occupied with fighting each other to send any troops to the peasant villages fighting for their lives in the ethnic cleansing. We will call them the Peasant Militia.

By November, Rome's 12th Legion had made its way to the city, which happened to be celebrating the Feast of Tabernacles. The Zealot Rebels attacked the legion, killing more than 500 and losing only 22 of their own men in that first campaign, and by month's end the 12th Legion suffered severe casualties. They were pursued in retreat, trapped in a mountain pass and dishonored when their standard (a pole topped with an eagle) was captured by the Zealot Rebel forces. This was a great humiliation to the Roman army. The standard, like our flag, was to be defended to the death. To have it stolen by the enemy was the ultimate disgrace. This single act, more than any other, ensured Jerusalem would suffer the full wrath of Rome.

After routing the enemy, the Jewish people spent the next few months struggling to build a new government. They divided the country into six regions. They appointed generals to lead the regions and minted new coins. The factions, who were not pro-Roman, built and fortified the wall around Jerusalem, built war machines, collected weapons, food, money and armor while training young recruits for the Roman retaliation that was guaranteed to come in response to the embarrassing defeat suffered in the November of 66.

Many took advantage of this reprieve. Tradition says Christians fled the city. They were obeying the Lord's warning made 33 years earlier.

Confusing isn't it? That's what discord and conflict does.

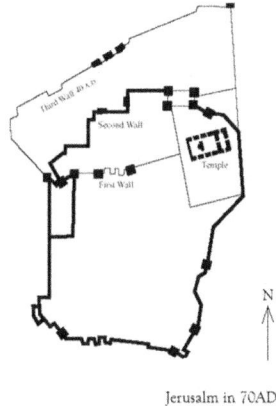

Jerusalm in 70AD

Even under the eminent threat of war, the city remained splintered three ways. Josephus devotes much of Books 4 and 5 of *Jewish Wars* to this second round of civil infighting. He describes it as "a wild beast grown mad, which...fell now upon eating its own flesh."[98]

The three Jerusalemite factions were led by Simon bar Giora, John of Gischala, and Eleazar bar Simon. Each faction began fighting the other two. In doing so, not only did they divide their forces and their leadership, but they did incredibly foolish things, such as burning their own food supplies.

There were three generals commanding three armies. The outermost and largest circuit of the walls was held by Simon [bar Giora], the middle of the city by John [of Gischala], and the Temple was guarded by Eleazar [bar Simon]. John and Simon were strong in numbers and equipment. Eleazar had the advantage of position: among these three there was constant fighting, treachery, and arson. The vast storehouse of grain was intentionally set on fire.

John got possession of the Temple by sending a party, under pretense of offering sacrifice, to slay Eleazar and his troops. This left the citizenry divided into two factions until the Romans were nearly upon them, and they joined forces against their common enemy[99].

Nero commissioned General Vespasian with the job of taking care of the Jewish uprising. Vespasian, commanding three legions marched on Jerusalem in the spring of 67. He knew of the infighting among the inhabitants of Jerusalem and determined to use their civil war to his advantage. He knew they would wear themselves down, making his objective easier to obtain. Time was on his side. By June of 68 he controlled Galilee, the coast and the Jordan valley. Able to attack from three sides, he was preparing to take the city when he got word that Nero Caesar had killed himself, leaving the throne without having appointed a successor. Vespasian abandoned the task at hand and headed back to Rome to lay claim to the throne.

Back in Rome, three other men were fighting among themselves to claim the throne: Galba, Vitellius, Otho. This caused Rome to enter into a civil war lasting a year. History calls it The Year of the Four Emperors. Three of the four throne-seekers were killed within weeks or months of being crowned. Vespasian finally emerged the victor. His first order of business: punish Jerusalem for humiliating Rome three years earlier. Vespasian sent his son, Titus, to finish the job he'd started.

While Rome was away and embroiled in their own civil war, the conflict in Jerusalem continued. John of Gaschala commanded his private army, Eleaser, son of Simon, led the Zealots. Simon bar Giora came on the scene as a self-proclaimed messiah. Three warring factions again!

Phase 3: The Great Siege[100]

Jesus knew exactly what he was talking about when he warned the people to flee immediately when they saw armies begin to surround the city[101]. Revelation Chapter 9 is a warning. It describes the siege in greater detail, which began during Passover of 70AD. John is seeing things that hadn't yet happened on the earth. Revelation Chapter 9 describes what will take place when the time for mercy expires and judgment is executed[102].

¹"Then the fifth angel blew his trumpet, and I saw a star that had fallen from the sky upon the earth. To this angel the key to the pit of the abyss was given,

²and he opened the pit of the abyss, and smoke like the smoke of a huge furnace puffed up out of the pit, and the sun and the air were darkened by the smoke from the pit.

³Out of the smoke came locusts upon the earth, but the power that was given to them was like the power of earthly scorpions.

⁴They were told not to injure the grass of the earth or any plant or tree, but only the people who did not have the mark of God's seal on their foreheads.

⁵They were not permitted to kill them, but only to torture them for five months, and the torture they inflicted was like the torture of a scorpion when it stings a man."

(Williams) Revelation 9:1- 5

In verse 2 we the sun is darkened by the smoke of the pit. If the prayers of the saints is likened to smoke rising from the altar of incense, does it not stand to reason that accusations and evil words originating from the kingdom of darkness would be likened to smoke as well? The smoke (evil, hate-filled words) shrouded the light (truth) and from that darkness came locusts. Locusts were the eighth Egyptian plague. Remember, Chapter 8 spoke of a plague on the sun.

Locusts, as anyone in the Middle East knows, can completely wipe out an entire year's food supply in no time. Locusts represent and speak of utter destruction, either by insects or armies. Their power was like scorpions, power in their tails. One of Rome's war machines was actually called a scorpion.

The locusts are Roman armies. But they are not coming for food supplies, as was often the primary objective in many of their campaigns. No, the sole purpose of this campaign was to destroy people. Who can escape this fate? Those

183

whose belong to God and have a mind to obey His warnings and honor His ways.

For 2,000 years the proof of the Covenant of Abraham was circumcision, but Jeremiah prophesied that the day would come when God would write His laws on human hearts and minds.

³³ "But this shall be the covenant that I will make with the house of Israel; After those days, saith the LORD, I will put my law in their inward parts, and write it in their hearts; and will be their God, and they shall be my people."

Jeremiah 31:33

¹⁴ "For as many as are led by the Spirit of God, they are the sons of God."

Romans 8:14.

How can John's readers avoid this horrible time of judgment? Heed God's words and warnings. Let His Spirit lead them.

What about the, 'not permitted to kill, but to torture for five months'? Let's look at the historical record of the siege.

General Titus, Vespasian's son, laid siege to the city on April 14, 70. Under his command were five Roman Legions, plus he was joined by the armies of at least five other small countries. The besieged didn't stand a chance.

Rome's first order of business was to break through the massive fortification walls that surrounded the city and the Temple. This took them the better part of five months to accomplish.

To seriously deplete the city's supplies, the General allowed worshippers to enter the city for Passover. Once inside the city walls, they were trapped. Titus refused to let them leave. Those who tried were crucified. Josephus reported that upwards of 500 people a day met this end. Starvation, disease and cannibalism resulted from the siege that began in April at Passover and resulted in the total destruction of the Temple five months later.

[6] **"In those days people will look for death but will not find it, they will long to die but death will flee from them."**

Revelation 9:6

There are accounts of starving people begging soldiers to kill them, but as a means of torture, to prolong the suffering, their requests were denied.

[7] "And the shapes of the locusts were like unto horses prepared unto battle; and on their heads were as it were crowns like gold, and their faces were as the faces of men.

[8] And they had hair as the hair of women, and their teeth were as the teeth of lions.

[9] And they had breastplates, as it were breastplates of iron, and the sound of their wings was as the sound of chariots of many horses running to battle."

Revelation 9:7-9

Revelation 9:7-10 gives John's readers a description of Roman Standard Bearers[103] as depicted on the Trajan Column. They are shown wearing skins of fierce animals: bears, lions, wolves, etc. The animal's skulls covered the standard bearer's heads as helmets.

Revelation 9:10-12 tells us:

- The length of time this woe would last- five months.
- Who Rome's actual king is[104]. The one really calling the shots in their global conquest is Satan, the destroyer.
- Warns of two more woes yet to come.

[10] **"... they had tails like scorpions with stings in them, so in their tails their power lay to injure men for five months.**

[11] **They had over them as king the angel of the abyss; in Hebrew he is called Abaddon,[105] in Greek, Apollyon.[106]**

[12] **The first woe is past. See! Two other woes are yet to come."**

Revelation 9:10-12

The city's three walls were breached, and the slaughter continued.

Revelation 9:13-21 describes the second woe.

[13] **"And the sixth angel sounded, and I heard a voice from the four horns of the golden altar which is before God,**

¹⁴ Saying to the sixth angel which had the trumpet, Loose the four angels which are bound in the great river Euphrates.

¹⁵ And the four angels were loosed, which were prepared for an hour, and a day, and a month, and a year, for to slay the third part of men.

¹⁶ And the number of the army of the horsemen were two hundred thousand thousand: and I heard the number of them.

¹⁷ And thus I saw the horses in the vision, and them that sat on them, having breastplates of fire, and of jacinth, and brimstone: and the heads of the horses were as the heads of lions; and out of their mouths issued fire and smoke and brimstone.

¹⁸ By these three was the third part of men killed, by the fire, and by the smoke, and by the brimstone, which issued out of their mouths.

¹⁹ For their power is in their mouth, and in their tails: for their tails were like unto serpents, and had heads, and with them they do hurt.

²⁰ And the rest of the men which were not killed by these plagues yet repented not of the works of their hands, that they should not worship devils, and idols of gold, and silver, and brass, and stone, and of wood: which neither can see, nor hear, nor walk:

²¹ Neither repented they of their murders, nor of their sorceries, nor of their fornication, nor of their thefts."

Revelation 9:13-21

A BIT OF JEWISH HISTORY BRINGS UNDERSTANDING

The King of Babylon, Nebuchadnezzar, set his sights on Jerusalem nearly 700 years before John's writing of Revelation. The city was destroyed, and the first Temple was burned to the ground.

After 70 years of exile and captivity, the people were granted permission to return home and rebuild. The boundary marker separating the Promised Land and the seat of the Babylonian Empire is the Euphrates River.[107]

When were these heavenly guards assigned this post at the Babylonian border? I don't know. What I do know, however, is that Jesus had not yet come.

The "seed of woman," which God promised back in Genesis, needed to step onto earth's stage, live a sinless life, die a sinner's death and crush the enemy's head. If the nation of Israel had been completely wiped out and the laws concerning blood sacrifice lost during the Babylonian Exile, or some other conquest, God's plan would have not been realized.[108]

I suspect the angels were stationed at the Euphrates at the time of the Babylonian exile.

189

When those heavenly sentries were released from their post, in verses 14-16, the wrath of hell was unleashed on Jerusalem and anyone found there. Satan's rage, pent up from the moment of his defeat by Christ's Death, Burial and Resurrection, explodes on a 450-acre piece of real estate.

The message of Satan's kingdom spews out like fire, clouds truth and is a toxic poison. It kills both coming and going. Do not take a ride on that horse! Those who do, are carried down a highway of destruction. They worship garbage that brings only death in their pursuit of things that end in death: murder, mysticism, immorality and thievery. Just like the image we are given in Genesis of two trees and the freedom to choose which principles man would live by, we have two choices today. Which kingdom's message will your life proclaim?

John laments in verse 21, "They never did repent of their murders, their practices in magic, their immorality, or their thefts." Words that are as wise today as they were back then.

Being Christ Followers, believers in His Covenant does not give anyone a license to live above the moral guidelines established by God. To be sealed of God means we give ourselves to know Him, trusting His ways and obeying His instruction. Nothing goofy or mystical or magical about it. The freedom to which Christ has made us free, gives us the ability to choose the King we wish to serve and honor by following His ways.

What if the Cross Changed Everything?

16

No More Delay

"...Alas! Alas! Alas for the inhabitants of the earth because of the remaining blasts of the three angels who are going to blow their trumpets!"

Revelation 8:13

That first trumpet blast dealt specifically with the Jewish nation and what happened on the judicial level. The second trumpet blast deals with all other nations and peoples and what happened on the judicial level.

John goes into detail about things that took place historically, touching on the heart of God to redeem all of mankind throughout all the earth. John describes how God's compassion reaches beyond the descendants of Abraham,

Isaac and Jacob. His intent has always been the redemption of all.

Revelation 10:1-7 lays the historical groundwork.

[1]"**Then I saw another mighty angel coming down from heaven. He was clothed in a cloud, with a rainbow over his head; his face was like the sun, his legs were like pillars of fire,**

[2] **and he had a little book open in his hand. He set his right foot on the sea and his left foot on the land,** [3]**and in a loud voice he shouted like the roaring of a lion; and when he had shouted, the seven thunders rumbled.**

[4]**When the seven thunders had rumbled, I was going to write it down, but I heard a voice from heaven say: "Seal up what the seven thunders have said, and do not write it down!"**

[5]**Then the angel, whom I had seen standing on the sea and on the land, raised his right hand to heaven,**

[6]**and swore by Him who lives forever and ever, who created the heavens and all that they contain, the earth and all that it contains, and the sea and all that it contains, that there should be no more delay,**

[7]**but in the days when the seventh angel speaks, when he is about to blow his trumpet, then God's mysterious message, in accordance with the good news He gave to His slaves, the prophets, would be accomplished."**

(Williams) Revelation 10:1-7

John is getting a view of history past. The rainbow references the covenant promise God made with Noah centuries before Abraham, Isaac, Jacob or Moses. The seven thunders is the perfected plan of God's redemption, hidden from everyone's view. No one knew the intricacies of that glorious plan. Some were given a glimpse here and there throughout history, but no one knew how those pieces would come together. No one saw it coming—not any man and certainly not the enemy.

ONE FOOT ON THE EARTH AND ONE ON THE SEA

This angel is charged with the things concerning the earth and its inhabitants. He is devoted completely to honor God and swears his allegiance to Him. This angel, like the four we saw earlier, has a specific mandate—also rooted in mercy—to hold back the execution of judgment, regardless of how guilty and deserving of the punishment humanity was. Mercy extends time.

Verse 7 warns the readers that the time of merciful delay—the stay of execution—is about to expire. Just before that happens, God's glorious plan is revealed! All that Christ

195

accomplished was made clearly evident. The Cross changed everything.

The Little Book

Just as the rainbow is the universal symbol of God's promise that never again would the entire earth be destroyed by flood waters. A universal message is contained in that little book in accordance with the phenomenal news of man's redemption by the blood of Jesus Christ.

[8] And the voice which I heard from heaven spake unto me again, and said, Go and take the little book which is open in the hand of the angel which standeth upon the sea and upon the earth.

[9] And I went unto the angel, and said unto him, Give me the little book. And he said unto me, Take it, and eat it up; and it shall make thy belly bitter, but it shall be in thy mouth sweet as honey.

[10] And I took the little book out of the angel's hand, and ate it up; and it was in my mouth sweet as honey: and as soon as I had eaten it, my belly was bitter.

[11] And he said unto me, Thou must prophesy again before many peoples, and nations, and tongues, and kings.

Revelation 10: 8- 11

John is given the commission to digest the simple truth contained in that book and to proclaim it to the world. All nations, languages and kings are to be informed that Satan has been stripped of his authority to control people through the laws of sin and death. Jesus has satisfied all those require-ments and has legal authority to establish a new government in the hearts of humanity. The law of love, built on grace and peace, takes preeminence over the previous laws.

This is certainly no small task! John accepts the commission. The word translated as 'bitter' also means keen and sharp. There are a few scenarios this image brings to mind, but in light of the urgency and importance of this message getting out; here is my take on what John is saying:

"This new message is sweet to hear, sweet to digest, sweet to speak. I took it in, digested it and it became a part of me. When that happened I could not keep it in! This message could not remain silent within me! I have to proclaim it. This message has become a driving force in my life as it will be in the lives of anyone who grasps its reality."

To navigate the legal loopholes of the laws of the kingdom of darkness, the previous covenant had been very involved and meticulous.

In Revelation 11:1-14

John sees how the Nation of Israel worked into God's plan.

¹And there was given me a reed like unto a rod: and the angel stood, saying, Rise, and measure the temple of God, and the altar, and them that worship therein.

Revelation 11:1

The measuring rod he is given does not measure distance. It measures time. Here again, the Hebrew mind thinks differently than does a Westerners.[109]

² "But the court which is without the temple leave out, and measure it not; for it is given unto the Gentiles: and the holy city shall they tread under foot forty and two months."

Revelation 11:2

This is a direct quote from Jesus when He answered the disciples question concerning His prophesy about the destruction of the Temple.

"And they shall fall by the edge of the sword, and shall be led away captive into all nations; and Jerusalem shall be trodden down of the Gentiles, until the times of the Gentiles be fulfilled."

Luke 21:24

What Does "Given to the Gentiles" Mean?

There are a few ideas out there, but the one that rings true in my view is referring to the centuries when the nation of Israel was ruled by foreign enemies—a period of time beginning in either in 721BC when the Assyrians conquered the Kingdom of Israel (The Northern Kingdom) or in 605BC when Babylon conquered the Kingdom of Judah (The Southern Kingdom). I lean toward 605BC simply because all the imagery of Revelation refers historically to the Southern Kingdom.

³"And I will give power unto my two witnesses, and they shall prophesy a thousand two hundred and threescore days, clothed in sackcloth.

⁴These are the two olive trees, and the two candlesticks standing before the God of the earth.

⁵And if any man will hurt them, fire proceedeth out of their mouth, and devoureth their enemies: and if any man will hurt them, he must in this manner be killed.

[6]These have power to shut heaven, that it rain not in the days of their prophecy: and have power over waters to turn them to blood, and to smite the earth with all plagues, as often as they will.

[7]And when they shall have finished their testimony, the beast that ascendeth out of the bottomless pit shall make war against them, and shall overcome them, and kill them.

[8]And their dead bodies shall lie in the street of the great city, which spiritually is called Sodom and Egypt, where also our Lord was crucified.

[9]And they of the people and kindreds and tongues and nations shall see their dead bodies three days and an half, and shall not suffer their dead bodies to be put in graves.

[10]And they that dwell upon the earth shall rejoice over them, and make merry, and shall send gifts one to another; because these two prophets tormented them that dwelt on the earth.

[11]And after three days and an half the Spirit of life from God entered into them, and they stood upon their feet; and great fear fell upon them which saw them.

[12]And they heard a great voice from heaven saying unto them, Come up hither. And they ascended up to heaven in a cloud; and their enemies beheld them.

[13]And the same hour was there a great earthquake, and the tenth part of the city fell, and in the earthquake were slain of men seven thousand: and the remnant were affrighted, and gave glory to the God of heaven.

[14]The second woe is past; and, behold, the third woe cometh quickly.

Revelation 11:3-14

John looks back through history and is made aware of the fantastic role the Jewish nation has played in the realization of God's plan. He also comes to realize that Jesus' grace, mercy, sacrifice and covenant were bigger than anyone's ability to comprehend or deserve.[110]

To understand the three and a half think of the seven-stemmed candlestick—the menorah with its center stem raised higher than the three stems flanking it. When you split the whole, perfectly down the middle there are three and a half stems. The center stem, which is intended to be the glorious joining of two opposites, is split and unable to shine.

Whenever the bible speaks in terms of three and a half, the Hebrew mind is on the lookout for the balancing complement. In this case the three and a half speaks of the time when God made a covenant with Abraham involving the temple, animal sacrifice, and strict obedience of the Jewish people at the exclusion of those outside that nation.

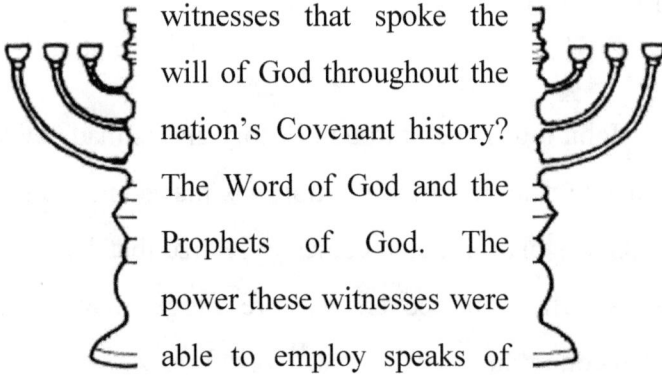

What are the two witnesses that spoke the will of God throughout the nation's Covenant history? The Word of God and the Prophets of God. The power these witnesses were able to employ speaks of the signs used by Moses (representing the laws of God) and the signs used by Elijah (representing the prophets of God). Both of these guiding factors were fueled by the power of God's Holy Spirit.

These two witnesses of God's truth were shrouded in death because of man's existence in the kingdom of death. These two witnesses are totally in line with the laws of death that govern the earth prior to the Cross: eye for an eye, sin demands blood in payment, required at the hand of the one who committed the sin. Is it any wonder why our Father's heart broke when we gave our allegiance to that system, as opposed to the one He had designed for us to enjoy?

In Matthew 5:17 Jesus said, *"Think not that I am come to destroy the law, or the prophets: I am not come to destroy, but to fulfill."*

The physical place responsible for maintaining the integrity of God's truth was Jerusalem and the Temple. The gentile world was completely oblivious to the gift with which the Jewish people had been entrusted. From the world's perspective, the Jewish nation was of no benefit or value. Celebration was in order whenever the world's ways struck a blow to these keepers of God's ways.

Verses 7-14 tell that the time came when these two witnesses completed their testimony. That era was marked by another three and a half split: Jesus' ministry culminating in His Death, Burial and Resurrection. Jesus embodied both parts of the Old Covenant. In John's gospel Chapters 10 and 18, we see where Jesus proclaims Himself and His works to be the two witnesses of truth.

These verses in Revelation 11 describe the events that took place when Jesus conquered hell and the grave. When the righteous dead were seen walking the streets of Jerusalem: Matthew 27:50-54.

The authentic, Spirit-Breathed Word of God are the two witnesses. These two witnesses, testifying the Truth of God's way and plan, were embodied in the Laws of God and the Prophecies of God. Then the time came when these two joined together and were found in one body—the body of Jesus Christ. When He rose from the grave, then ascended to Heaven, the power of the grave was broken. The nay-sayers and the unbelievers in Jesus as Messiah had changes of heart. These events proved He was Who He said He was, and that He accomplished what He set out to accomplish.

The Cross changed everything!

[15]**And the seventh angel sounded; and there were great voices in heaven, saying, The kingdoms of this world are become the kingdoms of our Lord, and of his Christ; and he shall reign forever and ever.**

[16]**And the four and twenty elders, which sat before God on their seats, fell upon their faces, and worshipped God,**

[17]**Saying, We give thee thanks, O Lord God Almighty, which art, and wast, and art to come; because thou hast taken to thee thy great power, and hast reigned.**

[18]**And the nations were angry, and thy wrath is come, and the time of the dead, that they should be judged, and that thou shouldest give reward unto thy servants the prophets, and to the saints, and them that fear thy name,**

small and great; and shouldest destroy them which destroy the earth.

[19]And the temple of God was opened in heaven, and there was seen in his temple the ark of his testament: and there were lightnings, and voices, and thunderings, and an earthquake, and great hail.

Revelation 11:15-19

Verses 15-19 again describe the earthshaking events that occurred at His Resurrection. The powers that governed the earth, rooted in the laws of sin and death, are dethroned. Jesus is exalted in the court of the universe. All of Heaven, who had been waiting on the execution of those laws, stand in absolute awe at the way God handled the situation! Humanity has been redeemed! The price of their ransom has been paid. The one who held them hostage to the demands of their law's dictates was suddenly unemployed.

17

It's Pivotal

Chiasm: Chiasmus (or chiasm) is a literary device in which two or more clauses are repeated in reverse order, and for which the inverted clauses may be either parallel to or in contrast to the corresponding clause in the first part of the chiasmus. For example: I am a good boy, and a good boy am I. This poetic device is used to emphasize the truth or importance of what's being said.

> *To display a chiastic structure, the text is sometimes presented in outline form, such as "A B C X C' B' A'", where the "X" represents the center of the chiasm. It is sometimes stated that the center of the chiasm marked a place of special emphasis...*[111]

John's gospel shows us that this literary form was his style of choice. There are fascinating studies on this subject, and I encourage you to explore them. A thoroughly satisfying start can be had by going to websites like the one referenced in the footnotes.[112] Search for the chiastic structure of John's epistles as well, and you will discover that John was a master at this literary form. It is a form well-suited to the Eastern way of thinking, which is very different than the Western mind. Westerners think in a linier fashion: this-then-this, then that-then-conclusion.

Most of my writing reflects this mind. I start an article off with something I hope intrigues a reader, then I attempt to keep them involved in the piece by giving them interesting tidbits along the path I hope to lead them on—until the culminating finale when my reader is pleased and satisfied for having given their time to the journey. The End.

This is not how the Hebrew writer writes because that is not how the Eastern mind thinks. Hebrew thought is focused on comparisons and contrasts, connecting the dots and coming full circle. The goal is to see the entire structure of a truth to gain wisdom and understanding. If you remember the menorah illustration a few chapters back, you can easily see the principle at work: for something to be fully illuminated, both halves must be considered and truth is found between the opposites. This is, by definition, a continuum—a continuous sequence in which adjacent elements are not perceptibly different from each other, although the extremes are quite distinct.

We Westerners have a tendency to want to 'cut to the chase' and not be bothered with those pesky details. But remember, John was not writing to a Western audience, nor had he a Western mindset.

Everyone appreciates the wisdom chiastic depth brings to a truth and immediately recognizes how anemic the half-truth was before the overlooked contrasting truth is revealed. For example:

"What counts is not necessarily the size of the dog in the fight, it's the size of fight in the dog."
Dwight D. Eisenhower.

"Mankind must put an end to war, or war will put an end to mankind."
John F. Kennedy.

"America did not invent Human Rights. In a very real sense it is the other way around. Human Rights invented America."

Jimmy Carter.

"By failing to prepare, you are preparing to fail."

Benjamin Franklin.

"The value of marriage is not that adults produce children, but that children produce adults."

Peter De Vries.

"The two most engaging powers of an author are to make new things familiar and make familiar things new."

Dr. Samuel Johnson.

It's easy to appreciate a good chiasm. A chiasm shows us the other side—a side to which we may have been blind. Recognizing the contrasting truth forces us to do one of two things: ignore the deeper truth or broaden our view to embrace it.

Another famous chiastic quote by John F. Kennedy is credited to have sparked the greatest move of volunteer service in the Nation's history. *"Ask not what your country can do for you. Ask what you can do for your country."* The people answered by joining the Peace Corps.

This literary structure is so powerful and persuasive because it covers both sides of a continuum. Revelation is a superb example, and though I've read many attempts at deciphering the riddle, I have yet to find a person, who includes in their outline any significant distinction between the previous Covenant and its Executor and the current Covenant and its new Executor.

REVELATION CHAPTER 12— JOHN SEES HOW GOD'S PLAN FITS INTO THE HISTORY OF THE HUMAN RACE

The woman represents all humanity throughout her history. It describes how Satan had set his sights on destroying mankind. Reference to "the third being removed" again speaks of the harmonizing factors being removed leaving chaos, conflict and confusion—an apt description of human history.

God's plan involved finding a person with whom He could enter into a universal agreement. That nation was found in Abraham and elevated that nation to a place of unparalleled distinction in all of humanity. Israel became the crown on the head of humanity.

Chapter 12 describes the historical battle waged by the enemy as it narrows in focus from mankind in general, to the nation of Israel, to the Tribe of Judah, to the house of David, to the town of Bethlehem, to the son of Mary, to the Cross of Calvary. John warns that the same vehemence continues to be poured out on those who hold the testimony of Jesus Christ.

VERSES 7-10 THE GREAT DEMOTION

When Christ fulfilled the requirements of the law, Satan, the universal score-keeping- fault-finding-persecuting-prosecuting accuser-of-humanity found himself without a job and no longer permitted access into the courts of heaven. He became obsolete. The authority he had been operating under since the time of Adam was the law of sin and death. And this was no longer the law of the land.

A new man, Jesus, had ushered in a new law.

Obsolete, archaic, unnecessary, purposeless—the accusations Satan spewed no longer held weight in the court of heaven. When Jesus exchanged his righteousness for our sin, no loopholes remained for Satan to exploit.

Satan was thrown out of heaven and confined to earth (God's footstool). The only audience he now has are also on the earth and consist solely of those who he is able to manipulate through deception.

Is the message of Revelation important to us today? Absolutely.

If we fail to grasp the finality of God's decision concerning these things, Satan is able (as has been the case for 2,000 years) to deceive and delude anyone unaware that he no longer holds any power, authority or rights over us because of sin.

Revelation 12:1-9 shows us yet another perspective: the tactics of the enemy on humanity throughout her history. The entire human race is represented by the woman. Israel holds a position of royal position and noble honor.

[1] And there appeared a great wonder in heaven; a woman clothed with the sun, and the moon under her feet, and upon her head a crown of twelve stars: [2]And she being with child cried, travailing in birth, and pained to be delivered.

[3]And there appeared another wonder in heaven; and behold a great red dragon, having seven heads and ten horns, and seven crowns upon his heads. [4]And his tail drew the third part of the stars of heaven, and did cast them to the earth: and the dragon stood before the woman

which was ready to be delivered, for to devour her child as soon as it was born.

⁵And she brought forth a man child, who was to rule all nations with a rod of iron: and her child was caught up unto God, and to his throne. ⁶And the woman fled into the wilderness, where she hath a place prepared of God, that they should feed her there a thousand two hundred and threescore days.

⁷And there was war in heaven: Michael and his angels fought against the dragon; and the dragon fought and his angels, ⁸And prevailed not; neither was their place found any more in heaven. ⁹And the great dragon was cast out, that old serpent, called the Devil, and Satan, which deceiveth the whole world: he was cast out into the earth, and his angels were cast out with him.

Revelation 12:1-9

One thousand two hundred and threescore days is just another way to say three and a half years. John is not likely talking about a literal period of time. Remember the menorah. This is half of a whole. What whole would that be? Human history. The half which existed under the first covenant. The completing half is presented in the next verses.

¹⁰ "And I heard a loud voice saying in heaven, Now is come salvation, and strength, and the kingdom of our God, and the power of his Christ: for the accuser of our

brethren is cast down, which accused them before our God day and night.

[11] **And they overcame him by the blood of the Lamb, and by the word of their testimony; and they loved not their lives unto the death."**

Revelation 12:10-11

Who are the 'they' verse 11 is talking about? They are the "declarers" from verse 10 of the new world order. Human beings are the only ones authorized to establish laws on the earth.

When did Jesus defeat our enemy? 2,000 years ago. When were humans set free from the bondage of sin and death? 2,000 years ago. When was humanity given authority to go throughout the earth and make disciples for the kingdom of God? 2,000 years ago. Why then are so many members of the body of Christ acting as if something else needs to happen before they can walk in the authority and privilege of Christ's New Covenant?

The accuser, deceiver, blinder of truth has focused his full attention on the inhabitants of the earth. His strategy for the past 2,000 years has been to deceive and keep as many humans as possible in the dark concerning his humiliating defeat and fall from power.

[12]Therefore rejoice, ye heavens, and ye that dwell in them. Woe to the inhabiters of the earth and of the sea! for the devil is come down unto you, having great wrath, because he knoweth that he hath but a short time.

[13]And when the dragon saw that he was cast unto the earth, he persecuted the woman which brought forth the man child.

[14]And to the woman were given two wings of a great eagle, that she might fly into the wilderness, into her place, where she is nourished for a time, and times, and half a time, from the face of the serpent.

[15]And the serpent cast out of his mouth water as a flood after the woman, that he might cause her to be carried away of the flood.

[16]And the earth helped the woman, and the earth opened her mouth, and swallowed up the flood which the dragon cast out of his mouth.

[17]And the dragon was wroth with the woman, and went to make war with the remnant of her seed, which keep the commandments of God, and have the testimony of Jesus Christ.

Revelation 12:12-17

Did you catch the Chiasm?

Revelation 12:6

"And the woman fled

    into the wilderness, where she has a place prepared by

    God,

        in which to be nourished

            1260 days

                        Revelation 12:14

            for three and one-half times.

        where she is to be nourished

    into the wilderness to the place

"And the woman was given the two wings of the great eagle

that she might fly from the serpent...

This is the pivotal concept of the entire book of Revelation: humanity before Christ, and humanity after His Cross.

These verses describe humanity's situation since the institution of the New Covenant. It is the completing half of her existence.

Jesus Christ is our Lord; Satan is not. Jesus took upon himself the entire debt, guilt, shame, price and punishment of our sin. He is our Savior; there remains no legitimate accusation with which Satan can hold us. Jesus has been given all authority in Heaven and Earth, and He, in turn has authorized us to take His authority and establish the Kingdom of Heaven on this Earth. What is that Kingdom? God's Spirit of love, joy and peace.

We have a job to do, and we are failing at it because we are cowering in our corners for fear of the future. A future that is being declared by well-intentioned speculators of 'end-time prophesies.'

In spite of the intentions what has happened is the body of Christ has been baptized in a perverted 'gospel' that questions salvation whenever Satan's agenda is exalted. That sort of message causes humans to remain blind to Christ's victory—as if the Cross didn't accomplish a single valid thing for us on this side of eternity.

Is the enemy out there? Yes. Does he have any legitimate authority to govern our lives and control our destiny? No! However, when we insist on remaining bound to the laws that previously governed the world; we do not experience the benefits of God's Kingdom. We remain locked in the prison of darkness.

18

Politics Is A Beast

The Beast

There is probably no portion of this document that has bred more speculation than Chapter 13, when in reality this is probably among the most clearly understood by the generation who first read it. This chapter of Revelation describes the politics of the Roman government.

The imagery and meanings used are well known to John's people. They come from the book of Daniel,[113] a man who prophesied during the Babylonian Exile as well as the Mede Persian conquest.

Daniel 7 beginning at verse 3:

And four great beasts came up from the sea, diverse one from another.
⁴ The first was like a lion, ...

This is Babylon.

⁵ And behold another beast, a second, like to a bear, and it raised up itself on one side, and it had three ribs in the mouth of it between the teeth of it: ...

This is Mede/Persia.

⁶ After this I beheld, and lo another, like a leopard, which had upon the back of it four wings of a fowl; the beast had also four heads; and dominion was given to it...

This is Greece.

⁷ After this I saw in the night visions, and behold a fourth beast, dreadful and terrible, and strong exceedingly; and it had great iron teeth: it devoured and brake in pieces, and stamped the residue with the feet of it: and it was diverse from all the beasts that were before it; and it had ten horns...

This final beast, unlike any that came before it, is Rome.

¹⁵ I Daniel was grieved in my spirit in the midst of my body, and the visions of my head troubled me.

16 I came near unto one of them that stood by, and asked him the truth of all this. So he told me, and made me know the interpretation of the things.

17 These great beasts, which are four, are four kings, which shall arise out of the earth.

The images describe, in order, the nations which conquered or would conquer Israel and Judea. When Daniel wrote this, they had already experienced the first two. John is writing during the reign of the fourth. This is no mystery to his readers. Let's see if we can demystify it for ourselves.

¹And I stood upon the sand of the sea, and saw a beast rise up out of the sea, having seven heads and ten horns, and upon his horns ten crowns, and upon his heads the name of blasphemy."

Revelation 13:1

The sand of the sea—another euphemism for the Jewish people[114]—John is looking at this from that perspective, and he sees a conquering nation rise from humanity. This beast had seven heads (leaders), ten horns (strength) and ten crowns (royal power).

Rome differed from previous kingdoms in its governing structure. For centuries, before Julius Caesar was crowned supreme sovereign over the entire kingdom, the empire was ruled by a senate. No one person could be singled out as being the 'head' of the Roman Empire. When Julius was crowned in 46BC Rome had its first recognizable 'head.'

How many 'heads' were there between Julius and the complete destruction of the Jewish Temple?

1. Julius
2. Augustus
3. Tiberius
4. Caligula
5. Claudius
6. Nero
7. Galba et al
8. Otho
9. Vitellius
10. Vespasian

Of these ten heads, only seven had enough time on the throne to lead or head the empire. 69AD was known as the year of the four Emperors. Caesars 7-10 ascended the throne just to be killed by another challenger. Vespasian eventually emerged as crowned victor and was seated on the throne as the 10th head of this beast called Rome.

[2] "And the beast which I saw was like unto a leopard, and his feet were as the feet of a bear, and his mouth

as the mouth of a lion: and the dragon gave him his power, and his seat, and great authority."

Revelation 13:2

These are the same animal images used by Daniel. John is saying that the present beast is a culmination of the previous three—Babylon's monarch-worship demands, the Mede/Persian cruelty and strength, and the Greek swiftness— all rolled into one. This conquering enemy is fueled by the principles that govern the kingdom of darkness. Satan is the motivator behind it all.

[3] **"And I saw one of his heads as it were wounded to death; and his deadly wound was healed: and all the world wondered after the beast."**

Revelation 13:3

Roman head number one, Julius Caesar, was killed in 44BC after reigning just two years. This sparked a civil war between those who wanted to continue with a monarchy and those who wanted to return to the senate-ruled government. This conflict lasted for years, and while the powers-that-be struggled to resolve the governing issue—single head or multiple senate voices—the world that Rome had conquered watched and wondered.

223

It took 13 years before the issue was settled. Rome crowned another Caesar. Life was breathed back into the monarchy after it had suffered the deadly wound.

⁴ "**And they worshipped the dragon which gave power unto the beast: and they worshipped the beast, saying, Who is like unto the beast? who is able to make war with him?**"

Revelation13:4

The beast, known as Rome, was worshipped and honored. The principles that governed Rome were worshipped and honored. It mattered not that his message was full of blasphemies against the True and Living God.

⁵ "**And there was given unto him a mouth speaking great things and blasphemies; and power was given unto him to continue forty and two months.**"

Revelation 13:5

There came a three-and-a-half-year period of time when this beast would exercise unparalleled force and power over God's chosen people.

⁶ "**And he opened his mouth in blasphemy against God, to blaspheme his name, and his tabernacle, and them that dwell in heaven.**

[7] "And it was given unto him to make war with the saints, and to overcome them: and power was given him over all kindreds, and tongues, and nations."

Revelation 13:6, 7

Because these gave their worship, honor and allegiance to the beast they empowered him.

[8] "And all that dwell upon the earth shall worship him, whose names are not written in the book of life of the Lamb slain from the foundation of the world."

Revelation 13:8

All who dwell on the earth, who worship the one whose name is not written the book of The Life of the Lamb-slain-since-the-world's-system-was-set.

[9] "If any man have an ear, let him hear."

Revelation 13:9

Pay attention!

[10] "He that leadeth into captivity shall go into captivity: he that killeth with the sword must be killed with the sword. Here is the patience and the faith of the saints."

Revelation 13:10

This one who led humanity into captivity will go into captivity. He kills with the sword and must suffer the same fate. Satan will suffer the fate he made others suffer. It's the merciless law he demanded be upheld that will judge him.

You can bank on it!

¹¹ "And I beheld another beast coming up out of the earth; and he had two horns like a lamb, and he spake as a dragon."
Revelation 13:11

As if one beast wasn't enough—here comes another of a different kind. This is a specific person—one who holds the power of Rome as a monarch and wields power over a second sphere as well.

¹² "And he exerciseth all the power of the first beast before him, and causeth the earth and them which dwell therein to worship the first beast, whose deadly wound was healed."
Revelation 13:12

Caesars were deified, and their worship was mandated by law. Can you imagine laws being passed in the United States demanding its citizens worship the Presidents as gods, and every election forced you to change the object of your worship? That was first-century reality.

¹³ "And he doeth great wonders, so that he maketh fire come down from heaven on the earth in the sight of men, ¹⁴ And deceiveth them that dwell on the earth by the means of those miracles which he had power to do in the sight of the beast; saying to them that dwell on the earth, that they should make an image to the beast, which had the wound by a sword, and did live."

Revelation 13:13, 14

The word translated 'miracle' is just as often translated 'sign.'. This doesn't have to be a supernatural exhibition of spiritual power.

¹⁵ "And he had power to give life unto the image of the beast, that the image of the beast should both speak, and cause that as many as would not worship the image of the beast should be killed."

Revelation 13:15

Again, this does not have to be supernatural demonstrations of power. This ruler exercised the power that Rome gave him. As a man exalted to the level of a god, Caesar's every whim was executed.

This Roman mouth-piece is connected to a great sign: fire. That fire was used as a sign of some sort to deceive the people, who live on the earth.

Nero, Caesar number six was on the throne in 64AD when 75% of the city of Rome burned to the ground. The Roman citizens accused him of intentionally setting the city on fire to make room for his next building project. Nero, in turn, blamed the Christians, and exterminated as many as he could of those who embraced the ways of Christ[115].

The following is from Flavius Tacitus, Roman Historian:

"Yet no human effort, no princely largess nor offerings to the gods could make that infamous rumor disappear that Nero had somehow ordered the fire. Therefore, to abolish that rumor, Nero falsely accused and executed with the most exquisite punishments those people called Christians, who were infamous for their abominations. The originator of the name, Christ, was executed as a criminal by the procurator Pontius Pilate during the reign of Tiberius; and though repressed, this destructive superstition erupted again, not only through Judea, which was the origin of this evil, but also through the city of Rome, to which all that is horrible and shameful floods together and is celebrated. Therefore, first those were seized who admitted their faith, and then, using the

*information they provided, a vast multitude were con-
victed, not so much for the crime of burning the city, but
for hatred of the human race. And perishing they were
additionally made into sports: they were killed by dogs
by having the hides of beasts attached to them, or they
were nailed to crosses or set aflame, and, when the day-
light passed away, they were used as nighttime lamps.
Nero gave his own gardens for this spectacle and performed a Circus game, in the habit of a charioteer mix-
ing with the plebs or driving about the race-course. Even
though they were clearly guilty and merited being made
the most recent example of the consequences of crime,
people pitied these sufferers, because they were consumed not for the public good but on account of the
fierceness of one man."*

[16] **"And he causeth all, both small and great, rich
and poor, free and bond, to receive a mark in their right
hand, or in their foreheads:** [17] **And that no man might buy
or sell, save he that had the mark, or the name of the beast,
or the number of his name."**

Revelation 13:16, 17

It is worth noting that although Judea was under the
rule of Rome, the Jewish people had been permitted to choose
their vocations, live their lives, farm their land, produce and
sell their wares. John is telling them that when this Emperor

229

makes this move, those freedoms would be abolished. Anyone surviving this tyrannical reign would become slaves.

John is warning his people regarding this powerful figure who demanded worship, killed at will and forced all to be marked for Rome, either as slaves or criminals.

What is the mark of this beast?

"Punitive tattooing continued into the Roman era. Julius Caesar, Cicero, Galen, and Seneca all mention tattoos (*stigmates*), and the Roman physician Aetius includes a description of tattoo application and tattoo removal as well as the formula for tattoo ink in his *Medicae artis principles*."[116]

"During the early Roman Empire, slaves exported to Asia were tattooed **"tax paid"**. Words, acronyms, sentences, and doggerel were inscribed on the bodies of slaves and convicts, both as identification and punishment. A common phrase etched on the forehead of Roman slaves was **"Stop me, I'm a runaway"**—evidence that the legionaries would have sported the tattoo on their hands. Aetius, the 6th century Roman doctor, recording that tattoos were found on the hands of soldiers.[117]"

Identifying the specific man John labels as a beast proved to be a simple task for a Hebrew reader:

[18] "Here is wisdom. Let him that hath understanding count the number of the beast: for it is the number of a man; and his number is Six hundred threescore and six."

Revelation 13:18

Wisdom Is the Practical Application of Truth.

Here, John warns, you must use wisdom. Not for figuring out the beast's identity, but to know what to do with the information they were being given. Those with understanding will know exactly who John's beast is. And those with wisdom will know what to do with that information.

Hebrew letters have specific numerical values. As do Roman numerals. 'I' is one, V is five, X is ten, etc. Another thing about the written Hebrew language is there are no markings for vowels.

Nero Caesar in Hebrew is NeRON QeiSaR; adding up the letters we get "the number of the man" 666.

נ	=	50
ר	=	200
ו	=	6
נ	=	50
ק	=	100
ס	=	60
ר	=	<u>200</u>
		666

The beast, clearly identified, is Nero.

19

Harvest Celebrations

In Revelation Chapter 14, John is given yet another perspective of the same event. Remember this is a courtroom. Many witnesses are called to give their testimony concerning the case being tried. John has recorded the testimonies of the signatories, the Covenant, Christ, the dead, the Nation of Israel, the Law and the Prophets, and human history. Now we will get the testimony of Christ, which is based on the imagery of the three annual Pilgrimage Festivals celebrated by the Jewish people.[118]

These three festivals were celebrated at the Temple in Jerusalem, and were to be attended by every able-bodied man each year. (Exodus 23:17) John knew that his readers were going to have to settle an issue. They had to know that God was okay with them not attending the celebrations, which for fifty generations had been mandatory. John had to communicate the fact that Jesus satisfied those obligations.

> [16] " *Three times a year shall all your males appear before the Lord your God in the place which He chooses: at the Feast of Unleavened Bread, at the Feast of Weeks, and at the Feast of Tabernacles or Booths. They shall not appear before the Lord empty-handed:*
> [17] *Every man* shall *give as he is able, according to the blessing of the Lord your God which He has given you.* "
>
> Deuteronomy 16:16-17

Festival #1 Passover (Pesach)

The Passover festival commemorated the Lord's deliverance of His people from Egypt and includes a ceremony to celebrate the early spring barley harvest. The special offering is received on the second day of this seven-day spring celebration.

Festival #2 Pentecost (Shavuot)

The second of the Three Pilgrim Festivals is a one-day celebration that falls in May or June. Shavuot means 'weeks' because it occurs 7 weeks after the 2nd day of Passover (50 days from the first). This festival marked the end of the wheat-grain harvest season and the beginning of the fruit harvest. A major feature of the celebration was the ceremony of bringing the "first fruits" of that year's yield to the Temple as an offering of thanksgiving.

Families gathered together singing and dancing while they walked to Jerusalem, carrying their food offerings. When they arrived at the Temple, they gave the bread and fruit to the priests to be blessed.

Festival #3 The Festival of Gathering or Tabernacles (Sukkot)

The Festival of Gathering or Tabernacles (Sukkot) is celebrated in Autumn, when the crops from the fields and the fruits of the orchards had been gathered. These events were celebrated with great excitement. Sukkot is also referred to as "The Time of Our Happiness." This festival celebrated the combination of both the spring and summer harvests.

WHAT DID JOHN SEE IN THE REALM OF HEAVEN THAT SPEAKS TO THESE JEWISH FESTIVAL CELEBRATIONS?

"And I looked, and, lo, a Lamb stood on the mount Sion, and with him an hundred forty and four thousand, having his Father's name written in their foreheads.

[2] And I heard a voice from heaven, as the voice of many waters, and as the voice of a great thunder: and I heard the voice of harpers harping with their harps: [3] And they sung as it were a new song before the throne, and before the four beasts, and the elders: and no man could learn that song but the hundred and forty and four thousand, which were redeemed from the earth.

[4] These are they which were not defiled with women; for they are virgins. These are they which follow the Lamb whithersoever he goeth. These were redeemed from among men, being the firstfruits unto God and to the Lamb. [5] And in their mouth was found no guile: for they are without fault before the throne of God.

[6] And I saw another angel fly in the midst of heaven, having the everlasting gospel to preach unto them that dwell on the earth, and to every nation, and kindred, and tongue, and people, [7] Saying with a loud voice, Fear God, and give glory to him; for the hour of his judgment is come: and worship him that made heaven, and earth, and the sea, and the fountains of waters."

Revelation 14:1-7

This is an image of the celebrations of Passover (The Lamb) and Pentecost—when the offering of first fruits are brought to Jerusalem. Every family brought their offering to the Temple, dancing and singing as they came.

In this case, the families didn't bring baskets filled with grains and fruits. No. This time the offering was people, who made the deliberate choice to honor God with their lives. We have seen these folks before in Revelation 7:4-8 when 12,000 from each of the 12 tribes were presented at the Throne of God.

The reference to them being virgins is not meant in a sexual sense. It means in a spiritual sense. These individuals have only ever served and worshipped the One True Living God. They have never spiritually strayed away from Him. Their obedience to that first Covenant has been rewarded and honored, and God has accepted them and the lives they lived as a pleasing offering and marked them as His own.

Somehow, their obedience satisfied a demand which enabled all to be ransomed. How that worked remains a mystery to me, but we do know that the families of Israel play an enormous role in God's plan. In some way, their numbers reckoned adequate and sufficient for the redemption of all people based on what we read in Deuteronomy.

"When the Most High gave to the nations their inheritance, when He separated the children *of men, He set the bounds of the peoples according to the number of the Israel-*

ites. For the Lord's portion is His people; Jacob (Israel) is the lot of His inheritance."

Deuteronomy 32:8-9

Proverbs 3 gives us a few hints concerning the value of honoring God with our lives and the firstfruits of our increase:

⁹ Honor the Lord with your capital and sufficiency [from righteous labors] and with the firstfruits of all your income;
¹⁰ So shall your storage places be filled with plenty, and your vats shall be overflowing with new wine.

Proverbs 3: 9, 10

We have a tendency to look at this principle in terms of the physical and economic, but it appears in Revelation to be operating on a spiritual and global scale, as well.

⁸ "And there followed another angel, saying, Babylon is fallen, is fallen, that great city, because she made all nations drink of the wine of the wrath of her fornication."

Revelation 14:8

Yes, Babylon is the first Empire on the list of conquering nations. However, this reference to Babylon is not that empire, nor is it referring to the ancient city. John uses numerous references from this point onward to Babylon, and it will become increasingly clear that he is referring to Jerusalem. Changing the name emphasize a change in character and function.

This is not without precedent. Throughout the Bible we see God giving people different names to reflect their character or purpose. The word Jerusalem literally means "teaching of peace." From what John is seeing in his vision, the things that are about to unfold in that city is anything but peace. It will be a horrific mix of confusion, chaos and conflict. A word that embodies those attributes is "Babylon," which means: mix, mingle, confuse and confound.

John's insistence on calling Jerusalem "Babylon" is to help reinforce this warning that the people must stay as far away from the city as possible.

[9] And the third angel followed them, saying with a loud voice, If any man worship the beast and his image, and receive his mark in his forehead, or in his hand, [10] The same shall drink of the wine of the wrath of God, which is poured out without mixture into the cup of his indignation; and he shall be tormented with fire and brimstone in the presence of the holy angels, and in the presence of the Lamb: [11] And the smoke of their torment ascendeth up forever and ever: and they have no rest day nor night, who

239

worship the beast and his image, and whosoever receiveth the mark of his name."

Revelation 14:9-11

SLAVES WERE MARKED ON THEIR FOREHEADS AND/OR FACES. SOLDIERS WERE MARKED ON THEIR HANDS.

If you have made a decision to devote your life to serving God and have accepted Christ's sacrifice for your redemption, you have been marked by the seal of the living God. Is that a physical mark? No. It is speaking symbolically of a spiritual reality. Just as a slave owner marked the foreheads of the people he enslaved identifying them as his property, John is reminding his readers that they too have been purchased by the One, who paid the ransom for their lives. Marked slaves were a common sight. John is using familiar imagery.

He wants to drive home the reality of their redemption by reminding them that the beasts (Rome and the reigning Caesar) though they demand worship, are not to be worshipped. Doing so will result in terrible consequences. Caesars are not to be worshipped as god, nor is it acceptable to serve Rome's military. Doing so would perpetuate Satan's principles and further the kingdom of darkness.

The following excerpt is from Military Institutions of the Romans, by Flavius Vegetius Renatus 390AD: "THE MILITARY MARK"

"The recruit, however, should not receive the military mark[119] as soon as enlisted. He must first be tried if fit for service; whether he has sufficient activity and strength; if he has capacity to learn his duty; and whether he has the proper degree of military courage. For many, though promising enough in appearance, are found very unfit upon trial. These are to be rejected and replaced by better men; for it is not numbers, but bravery which carries the day.

After their examination, the recruits should then receive the military mark…"

12 Here is the patience of the saints: here are they that keep the commandments of God, and the faith of Jesus.

Revelation 14:12

"The patience of the saints," translation: Here is a clear instruction for those who desire to serve and honor God and His kingdom: do not swerve from your deliberate purpose by giving your loyalty, service or faith away even when met by the greatest of trials and suffering.

¹³ "And I heard a voice from heaven saying unto me, Write, Blessed are the dead which die in the Lord from henceforth: Yea, saith the Spirit, that they may rest from their labours; and their works do follow them."

Revelation 14:13

From here on out, those who abide in Christ are blessed—even in death. God's Spirit agrees; no longer are blessings attached to self-effort and obedience to the sacrificial system. The Cross has made it possible for man to rest from those laborious demands. Works now follow after men, rather than being the thing that paved their way.

The Cross changed everything!

Why is it important for the people to know this? Under the first covenant, God's ability to pour blessings into the lives of His people was limited by their observance of ritual and ceremony. Under the laws of this New Covenant, Jesus has fulfilled those pilgrimage festival requirements.

¹⁴ "And I looked, and behold a white cloud, and upon the cloud one sat like unto the Son of man, having on his head a golden crown, and in his hand a sharp sickle.

242

¹⁵ And another angel came out of the temple, crying with a loud voice to him that sat on the cloud, Thrust in thy sickle, and reap: for the time is come for thee to reap; for the harvest of the earth is ripe[120]. ¹⁶ And he that sat on the cloud thrust in his sickle on the earth; and the earth was reaped."

Revelation 14:14-16

Once Christ satisfied the requirements for the Passover celebration the earth's true harvest (humanity) began. John observes the second festival, Pentecost and First Fruits as it is being celebrated in heaven.

¹⁷ "And another angel came out of the temple which is in heaven, he also having a sharp sickle.

¹⁸ And another angel came out from the altar, which had power over fire; and cried with a loud cry to him that had the sharp sickle, saying, Thrust in thy sharp sickle, and gather the clusters of the vine of the earth; for her grapes are fully ripe.

¹⁹ And the angel thrust in his sickle into the earth, and gathered the vine of the earth, and cast it into the great winepress of the wrath of God."

Revelation 14:17-19

Who is the vine? Recorded in John 15:5, Jesus calls Himself the vine. The vine is cut down and cast into the winepress of the wrath of God. John wrote in two of his

243

epistles about the concept of propitiation. Propitiation is the appeasement of wrath and reconciliation of relationship.

JESUS SATISFIED THE LAST FESTIVAL AS WELL.

The Ingathering was a celebration made all the more exuberant by the newly fermented grape harvest.

^{20} " And the winepress was trodden without the city, and blood came out of the winepress, even unto the horse bridles, by the space of a thousand and six hundred[121] furlongs."

Revelation 14:20

Christ was crucified at Golgotha—a place located just outside the walls of the city. The number 1,000 means absolute completion. The number 6 is always used in connection to work, performance, and duty. Christ's blood satisfies the time when it was dependent on man's ability, in the flesh, to make the Old Covenant. His blood is what the messengers would pass through, when they proclaimed this magnificent message to the world. A message that announces the absolute completion (1,000) of man's necessity to work, perform (600) to enjoy salvation.

"For what the law [Old Covenant] could not do, in that it was weak through the flesh, God sending his own Son in the likeness of sinful flesh, and for sin, condemned sin in the flesh."

Romans 8:3

The instructions for celebrating the Feast of Tabernacles is found in Deuteronomy 16, beginning with verse 13.

"Celebrate the Feast of Tabernacles for seven days after you have gathered the produce of your threshing floor and your winepress. Be joyful at your Feast—you, your sons and daughters, your menservants and maidservants, and the Levites, the aliens, the fatherless and the widows who live in your towns. For seven days celebrate the Feast to the LORD your God at the place the LORD will choose. For the LORD your God will bless you in all your harvest and in all the work of your hands, and your joy will be complete."

Deuteronomy 16:13-15

What is God's instruction for this feast? Celebrate with food and wine. Celebrate with family, friends and strangers. Celebrate with joy. Celebrate for seven days. Celebrate God's blessing of all your harvest, all your increase, all your work and satisfies your joy.

That is quite a celebration! Jesus, thank you for the Cross. It changed everything!

20

Croaks & Plagues

The Warning Intensifies. The Reason Made Clear.

If the theory of this book—showing how Jesus initiated and completed this covenant—holds true, what John is
describing are the final events marking the completion of the
covenant God made with the people of Israel when they
accepted the responsibilities that came with receiving His
laws.

In those laws, God made provision for how the people
were to conduct themselves and ~~take~~ advantage of oversights
in the enemy's garrison and create openings. These openings
enabled God to slip as much grace and mercy into the earth

and onto people as was Heavenly possible. The size of those openings were determined by how closely the people followed His instructions. Was that God's original plan? No! But, it was the best that could be offered under the circumstance.

Life or Death? Blessing or Curse?

By the time Abraham's family had spent 400 years enslaved in Egypt, they had grown into a full-fledged nation. Moses led them out from under that existence with every intention to lead them into the land of promised blessing. That plan fell through. They needed 40 more years spent training a generation capable of trusting God and His provision. Those years were also used to establish the system of blood animal sacrifice used in atoning for sin.

God's promised Seed[122] had to get to the Cross if man were ever going to be set free. The stakes were mind-numbingly high. The articles and limits of the covenant were clearly defined. "If you do this, I will be able to bless and prosper you." "Walk in this way and under these laws; if you refuse to stay within the boundaries of this agreement you will—by default—be walking head-long into the enemy's trap. And all hell will break loose." Could He make it any more clear? Rejecting God and the provision He was able to make secured their defeat.

Covenant agreements have both blessings and curses attached to them.[123] These made with Israel are no exception. Read Deuteronomy 28:15-68 and Leviticus 26:14-39 for a very clear description of the devastating effects of walking out from under the protection provided by being in covenant relationship with God.

All the people were made fully aware of the benefits that they could expect when walking within the boundaries of the partnership, as well as the dangers they would be facing when walking outside those clearly defined boundaries. The people acknowledged that they understood and agreed with the attached conditions.

It is very hard for us to wrap our minds around the idea of blessings and curses. It is not a part of our everyday lives. The closest we might come to grasping this principle is reward and punishment.

Life before the covenant of Christ was an inescapable existence under the bondage of the world's tyrannical dictator and the laws that existence demanded was never God's idea. We were the ones who bought into it.

The series of covenants God initiated with men made it possible—over the course of 4,000 years—to defeat the ruler of that governing mountain—a feat that could only be realized within the confines of the governing laws.

With That Said, Let's Explore Revelation Chapters 15 and 16

Revelation Chapter 15 describes the messengers as they prepare to execute a judgment against a specific criminal act. Which one? The events that complete the judgment made when that crowd—30 some odd years earlier—had cried out "Crucify Him! Let His blood be on us and on our children!"

John sees seven messengers—each one responsible for the execution of a specific aspect of the agreed-upon judgments connected to the breaking of a covenant. To separate from The Source of Life, Light and Love automatically creates an environment of death, darkness, chaos, self-centeredness, hate and fear—a perfect description of what transpires when Nero orders the destruction of the Jewish Nation.

¹ And I saw another sign in heaven, great and marvelous, seven angels having the seven last plagues; for in them is filled up the wrath of God.

² And I saw as it were a sea of glass mingled with fire: and them that had gotten the victory over the beast, and over his image, and over his mark, and over the number of his name, stand on the sea of glass, having the harps of God.

³ And they sing the song of Moses the servant of God, and the song of the Lamb, saying, Great and marvelous are thy works, Lord God Almighty; just and true are thy ways, thou King of saints.

⁴ Who shall not fear thee, O Lord, and glorify thy name? for thou only art holy: for all nations shall come and worship before thee; for thy judgments are made manifest.

⁵ And after that I looked, and, behold, the temple of the tabernacle of the testimony in heaven was opened:

⁶ And the seven angels came out of the temple, having the seven plagues, clothed in pure and white linen, and having their breasts girded with golden girdles.

⁷ And one of the four beasts gave unto the seven angels seven golden vials full of the wrath of God, who liveth forever and ever.

⁸ And the temple was filled with smoke from the glory of God, and from his power; and no man was able to enter into the temple, till the seven plagues of the seven angels were fulfilled.

Revelation 15:1-8

251

Revelation Chapter 16 describes the horrible consequences of that fateful decision to reject God's Messiah. The
terminology and imagery John uses is very familiar to a Jewish
audience. They speak of a specific, defining, chapter in
history—their deliverance from Egypt.

The Egyptians had suffered with: boils, water turned
to blood, darkness, frogs[124] and pain. Those first-century
readers knew exactly what was being communicated. Heed
this warning now! Why? Those curses, clearly laid out, and
universally agreed upon, are going to be unbearable.

The events transpired over the course of a literal three
and a half years,[125] prior to the fulfillment of Christ's prophecy
concerning those who demanded His crucifixion, the city of
Jerusalem and the Temple in 70AD.

- **SPRING 66** The injustices and greed that mark Flores'
  governorship spark the Jewish revolt.

- **AUTUMN OF 66** Nero commissions one of his top
  generals, Vespasian, to take control of the Jewish uprising.

- **WINTER OF 66** Vespasian with his son, Titus begin the
  campaign. Vespasian commands two legions, Titus leads a
  third. The total number of troops is roughly 60,000.

•   **SPRING OF 67** The legions arrive in Galilee.

The region of Galilee is north-west of Jerusalem, and the valley of Megiddo is part of that Galilee. The 'battle of Armageddon' is a phrase many people are familiar with, when asked, most would say it's earth's final battle. Whether you choose a historical or futuristic paradigm of interpretation of the book of Revelation, the battle is described as the one that precedes the battle that destroys Jerusalem. Archeologist, Eric Cline brings this out in his book, Battles of Armageddon. "Contrary to popular belief, the battle scheduled to be fought at Armageddon is in fact to be not the last battle ever fought, but rather the penultimate one, taking place during the first phase of the final conflict...Then is the battle at Jerusalem." [126]

The historical account by Josephus describes the carnage suffered when Rome marched through on its way to Jerusalem. "Galilee from end to end became a scene of fire and blood; from no misery, no calamity was it exempt; the one refuge for the hunted inhabitants was in the cities fortified by Josephus." [127]

- **JULY OF 67** The first heavily fortified city Jotapata is taken. 40,000 citizens killed. 1,200 women and infants captured.

- **AUGUST-SEPTEMBER 67** The second major fortified city Tarichaeae is taken.

- **SEPTEMBER 26, 67** The non-rebels of the city of Tarichaeae were 'granted permission' to leave the city. They are led to the stadium at Tiberias (about 5 miles away) where 1,200 were slaughtered, 6,000 youths were selected to be sent to Nero, and 30,400 were sold into slavery or given to King Agrippa. Most all of Galilee surrendered at this time.

- **AUTUMN 67** The legions move on to the third fortified city, Gamala.

- **NOVEMBER 10, 67** Gamala ends with 4,000 citizens killed and 5,000 committing suicide by jumping into a ravine. Only 2 women were spared this slaughter. They were nieces of one of Agrippa's commanders. The last 'rebellious' city in Galilee, Gischala, was taken. Of those caught attempting to escape to Jerusalem, 6000 men were killed, 3000 women and children captured.

- **WINTER 68** Vespasian begins conquering Judean cities. He is in no hurry to get to Jerusalem because of the infighting.

The people inside the city walls are destroying one another at an alarming rate.

- **SPRING 68** General Placidus takes Eastern Judea from Gadara to the Dead Sea. 15,000 are slaughtered and 2,200 captured. "So many were swept into the river that even the Dead Sea filled with bodies," reported Josephus.[128] Jewish deserters are used to beef up the Roman army, forcing them to kill their own people.

- **JUNE 68** Vespasian has Jerusalem completely isolated when he learns of Nero's suicide.

- **WINTER 68/69** The campaign is suspended, awaiting orders from the new Caesar, Galba, concerning the Jews and Jerusalem.

- **JANUARY 69** Galba is assassinated. He is succeeded by Otho.

- **APRIL 69** Otho is killed in the civil war.

- Vitellious is declared Emperor by his armies, at the same time Vespasian is declared Emperor by his.

- **DECEMBER 21, 69** Vitellious is murdered by a mob.

- **DECEMBER 22, 69** Vespasian is declared Emperor. He leaves for Rome and charges Titus with the job of finishing the march against Jerusalem.

- **SPRING 70** Titus surrounds Jerusalem. The siege begins. It lasts 5 months until August of that year when everything and everyone are conquered.

REVELATION 16 IS A DESCRIPTION OF WAR

[1] "And I heard a great voice out of the temple saying to the seven angels, Go your ways, and pour out the vials of the wrath of God upon the earth.

[2] And the first went, and poured out his vial upon the earth; and there fell a noisome and grievous sore upon the men which had the mark of the beast, and upon them which worshipped his image.

[3] And the second angel poured out his vial upon the sea; and it became as the blood of a dead man: and every living soul died in the sea.

[4] And the third angel poured out his vial upon the rivers and fountains of waters; and they became blood.

[5] And I heard the angel of the waters say, Thou art righteous, O Lord, which art, and wast, and shalt be, because thou hast judged thus.

[6] For they have shed the blood of saints and prophets, and thou hast given them blood to drink; for they are worthy.

[7] And I heard another out of the altar say, Even so, Lord God Almighty, true and righteous are thy judgments.

[8] And the fourth angel poured out his vial upon the sun; and power was given unto him to scorch men with fire.

⁹ **And men were scorched with great heat, and blasphemed the name of God, which hath power over these plagues: and they repented not to give him glory."**

Revelation 16:1-9

Verse 9 tells us that even under these conditions people refused to repent and give God glory—the glory due Him for constructing His magnificent plan. Verse 11 says they also refused to repent of their deeds. These statements indicate that even in these dire circumstances, before the precipice, God would gladly have extended forgiveness and welcomed them into the grace and peace made available to them in the New Covenant.

¹⁰ **"And the fifth angel poured out his vial upon the seat of the beast; and his kingdom was full of darkness; and they gnawed their tongues for pain,**

¹¹ **And blasphemed the God of heaven because of their pains and their sores, and repented not of their deeds.**

¹² **And the sixth angel poured out his vial upon the great river Euphrates; and the water thereof was dried up, that the way of the kings of the East might be prepared.**

¹³ **And I saw three unclean spirits like frogs come out of the mouth of the dragon, and out of the mouth of the beast, and out of the mouth of the false prophet.**

¹⁴ **For they are the spirits of devils, working miracles, which go forth unto the kings of the earth and of the**

whole world, to gather them to the battle of that great day of God Almighty."

Revelation 16:11-14

At the time the sixth blow was struck, John sees three unclean spirits—like frogs—come out of the mouths of the dragon (Satan), the beast (Rome or Nero) and the false prophet (possibly Nero's appointed Governor of Judea, Flores, if not Nero himself). When something comes out of a mouth, be it a sharp, two-edged sword proclaiming truth or a croaking frog, the imagery is about the quality of the words pouring out of those mouths. What comes out of the mouths of these three are connected to the curse.

¹⁵ **"Behold, I come as a thief. Blessed is he that watcheth, and keepeth his garments, lest he walk naked, and they see his shame."**

Revelation 16:15

Verse 15 makes little sense to us, yet again it was perfectly clear to the first-century readers. The Lord continued to extend grace and mercy. He was telling anyone who'd listen that He desires them to return to a covenant relationship.

A 'thief in the night' refers to a groom returning to claim his betrothed and take her with him to the place he has prepared.[129] The reference to garments is also connected to the wedding ceremony. When the bridegroom arrived, in the dark of night to steal away his bride, she had only time enough to grab a lamp and her clothes.

This seems out of place in the narrative, but in light of Christ's desire that none should perish, but all come to accept the redemption made available to them, it is perfectly situated. The invitation to join this covenant—likened to a marriage covenant—is still open, even in these final moments before the execution of judgment.

[16] "And he gathered them together into a place called in the Hebrew tongue Armageddon."

Revelation 16:16

The demonically motivated words gathered their forces together in the place called, in Hebrew, Armageddon. This is the first and only time the word 'Armageddon' is used in the Bible.

There was an ancient city called Megiddo[130] that stands at the edge of the Jezreel Valley. This region is what Vespasian, Titus, Agrippa and other enemies of Israel spent most of the year 68 destroying—the Galilean cities of the Jezreel Valley.

However, there was no physical place called Armageddon. This indicates John is throwing out another clue. It seems that by stipulating this word be understood by Hebrew definition, he is encouraging a focus on its meaning, rather than trying to pinpoint a geographical location.

WHAT DOES IT MEAN?

Armageddon is a compound word made of two Hebrew words: "mountain" and "place of crowds."[131]

Was there a time and place when a crowd became a governing authority ruled by pride[132] and arrogance? Yes. It was a crowd that demanded Jesus be crucified, the sheer mass of them pushing the governing leaders—Pontius Pilate and Herod—to consent to their demand. And where did that incident take place? Jerusalem. The result of that decision— made by the pride-filled mod— universally shook the government of earth.

¹⁷ And the seventh angel poured out his vial into the air; and there came a great voice out of the temple of heaven, from the throne, saying, it is done."

Revelation 16:17

Verse 17 ends with the words, "It is done." Meaning it has come to pass. What has come to pass? The final blow that will put an end to the sacrificial system once and for all. John is, from his vantage point, looking forward to the time when Jerusalem will be required to pay for the gross injustices against God's servants, His Word, His Prophets, their Messiah and His Son. John sees the prescribed end of the great city and her magnificent Temple.

¹⁸ "And there were voices, and thunders, and lightnings; and there was a great earthquake, such as was not since men were upon the earth, so mighty an earthquake, and so great.
¹⁹ And the great city was divided into three parts, and the cities of the nations fell: and great Babylon came in remembrance before God, to give unto her the cup of the wine of the fierceness of his wrath.
²⁰ And every island fled away, and the mountains were not found.
²¹ And there fell upon men a great hail out of heaven, every stone about the weight of a talent: and men

blasphemed God because of the plague of the hail; for the plague thereof was exceeding great."

Revelation 16:18-21

Jerusalem and the Temple are completely destroyed. There is a great shift in the foundations of the earth, greater than has ever been accomplished on the earth before or since. Great blows of judgment fall on the city, which was literally divided into three warring factions. The city remains divided into three religious factions to this day: Christians, Jews, and Muslims.

The last vestiges of the laws involved with humanity's righteousness are complete. There are no remnants remaining, nor can the accuser continue to build cases against humans on the basis of their sin separating them from the life of God. That system has been made completely obsolete. The Cross changed everything for everyone!

21

Brides, Beasts, Horns & Harlots

John has been given a front-row seat to the greatest court proceedings in all of history. He saw witnesses from the past be called to testify in the present, and he was permitted to view the future. From where he stood historically (possibly 64-65AD) when writing this, the war symbolized by the bowls and plagues was a future event. Where we stand historically, those events are past.

Chapters 17 to 19

Revelation Chapters 17-19 goes into more detail explaining how the broken promises of the first Covenant and the rejection of a belief in Christ as the fulfillment of that Covenant, was the cause of that devastation. An angelic

263

translator helped John make sense of the symbolic imagery of the judgment involving a great harlot, seated on many waters.

[1] **"And there came one of the seven angels which had the seven vials, and talked with me, saying unto me, Come hither; I will shew unto thee the judgment of the great whore that sitteth upon many waters: [2] With whom the kings of the earth have committed fornication, and the inhabitants of the earth have been made drunk with the wine of her fornication.**

[3] So he carried me away in the spirit into the wilderness: and I saw a woman sit upon a scarlet coloured beast, full of names of blasphemy, having seven heads and ten horns.

[4] And the woman was arrayed in purple and scarlet colour, and decked with gold and precious stones and pearls, having a golden cup in her hand full of abominations and filthiness of her fornication: [5] And upon her forehead was a name written, MYSTERY, BABYLON THE GREAT, THE MOTHER OF HARLOTS AND ABOMINATIONS OF THE EARTH.

[6] And I saw the woman drunken with the blood of the saints, and with the blood of the martyrs of Jesus: and when I saw her, I wondered with great admiration."

Revelation 17:1-6

The messenger reveals the mystery—in a very mysterious manner. It's time to get out our secret decoder ring.

- Beast—Rome/Nero
- Heads—Rulers
- Horns—Power/Authority/Force

Here is my stab at the meaning of that translation:

This one, who had been the promised bride, chose instead to join herself to another.[133] She presented herself to a watching world as one who was faithful to her betrothed, but she is not. She lords over many, many people, and the throne upon which she sits gets its power from the fear of bloodshed, which is the foundation for the kingdom of darkness, of which Rome is a part. She pretends to be the queen, faithful to her betrothed King, but she is in fact a branded slave. Her appetite for the blood of God's true covenant-keepers impaired her judgment to comprehend truth.

[7] **"And the angel said unto me, Wherefore didst thou marvel? I will tell thee the mystery of the woman, and of the beast that carrieth her, which hath the seven heads and ten horns.**

[8] **The beast that thou sawest was, and is not; and shall ascend out of the bottomless pit, and go into perdition: and they that dwell on the earth shall wonder, whose names were not written in the book of life from the foundation of the world, when they behold the beast that was, and is not, and yet is.**

[9] "And here is the mind which hath wisdom. The seven heads are seven mountains, on which the woman sitteth.

[10] And there are seven kings: five are fallen, and one is, and the other is not yet come; and when he cometh, he must continue a short space.

[11] And the beast that was, and is not, even he is the eighth, and is of the seven, and goeth into perdition.

[12] And the ten horns which thou sawest are ten kings, which have received no kingdom as yet; but receive power as kings one hour with the beast.

[13] These have one mind, and shall give their power and strength unto the beast.

[14] These shall make war with the Lamb, and the Lamb shall overcome them: for he is Lord of lords, and King of kings: and they that are with him are called, and chosen, and faithful.

[15] And he saith unto me, The waters which thou sawest, where the whore sitteth, are peoples, and multitudes, and nations, and tongues.

[16] And the ten horns which thou sawest upon the beast, these shall hate the whore, and shall make her desolate and naked, and shall eat her flesh, and burn her with fire.

[17] For God hath put in their hearts to fulfill his will, and to agree, and give their kingdom unto the beast, until the words of God shall be fulfilled.

[18] And the woman which thou sawest is that great city, which reigneth over the kings of the earth."

Revelation 17:7-18

The beast, upon which the Jewish leaders in Jerusalem sit, is Rome. It has (will have by the time of Jerusalem's destruction) seven recognized rulers heading its empire. Rome, the capitol city of that empire, is literally built around seven mountains. The beast refers to the Empire, its Emperors and the city itself.

The beast that previously was, presently is not, and yet is. What does that mean? Hang on it's about to become very clear.

There are seven kings.

The 'Five have fallen':

1) Julius

2) Augustus

3) Tiberius

4) Caligula

5) Claudius

The 'One is':

6) Nero

The 'Other has not yet come':

7) Vespasian

And when he (Vespasian) comes there will be a short time of waiting. That was the year of the four emperors. It took a while for the dust to settle and Vespasian to get his Caesar crown.

The beast that was, and is not, is himself also the eighth Caesar. He is of Caesar number seven.

Any idea who Caesar number eight was? Vespasian's son, Titus. The very same Titus that oversaw Jerusalem's fall. He literally came from Caesar number seven.

The ten horns (verse 12) are ten kings, who have never ruled a kingdom, but Rome gives them brief stints in positions of authority.

Any idea how many Rome-appointed governors there were between the time of Christ's crucifixion and the fall of Jerusalem?

Rome-Appointed Governors of Judea from The Cross to the end of animal sacrifice at the Temple:

1. Pontius Pilate
2. Marcellus
3. Marullus
4. Cuspius Fadus
5. Tiberius Alexander

6. Ventidius Cumanus
7. Felix
8. Festus
9. Albinus
10. Florus

Yep—ten. These rulers, stationed in Jerusalem, fully embraced the Roman ideals and did nothing to further the kingdom of Heaven, ushered in by the Sacrifice of Christ, although they too were aware of the things that had taken place in that city. They—like the Jewish leaders—when presented with the offer of redemption under the New Covenant rejected Christ. They chose instead, to fight against everything God's Kingdom stands for.

She sits on the power the Roman Governors allow her, but they, in fact, hate her. Who is she? She is Jerusalem and the leaders seated there who used their positions of leadership for selfish motives and to deceive others. She has sacrificed her true ordained power and authority given her by God at the altar of illegitimate force and power that Rome embodies.

Revelation 18 continues to describe the effects of Jerusalem's complete destruction as it is perceived through the

269

eyes of the watching world. A world that had come to believe the city's only value to them was for economic gain. That's a far cry from God's hope that the world would come to know His love and redemption.

Verse 4 inserts another plea for all who dwell in the city to leave. Warning that anyone who remains will suffer what is about to take place.

Verses 23-24

God's desire was for His people to represent Him in such a way that all nations would want to know Him, that all people would be invited to share in the plan of salvation and experience the freedom of knowing Him. What happened instead was that all nations were deceived into thinking that God had rejected them and had no plan for anyone outside the nation of Israel. Anyone who proclaimed that or any other truth contrary to the accepted interpretation of Scripture, namely the prophets and the saints, were killed. The city was held responsible not only for encouraging and approving of the deaths of those proclaimers-of-truth, but for everyone who died not having heard that truth.

Revelation 19

Those present in the court of Heaven agree with the reasoning upon which this judgment rests. The multitude (Angels) concurs. The twenty-four elders (legal counsel) concur. The four living creatures (representing earth's physical realm) concur.

This is commemorated and celebrated with singing a song of praise to God by the great multitude (the redeemed). The song they sing, declaring this earthshaking truth is:

"Alleluia! For the Lord God Omnipotent reigns! Let us be glad and rejoice and give Him glory, for the marriage of the Lamb has come, and His wife has made herself ready. And to her (His bride) it was granted to be arrayed in fine linen, clean and bright, for the fine linen is the righteous acts of the saints."

This image highlights the contrast between the first betrothed, forever stained by the blood of the murdered righteous and the bride clothed in the beautiful righteous acts of those saints.

271

GOD ISSUES HIS RULING ON THE MATTER OF SATAN VS. HUMANITY

[9] "Then he said to me, "Write: 'Blessed are those who are called to the marriage supper of the Lamb!'" And he said to me, "These are the true sayings of God."

Revelation 19:9

CELEBRATION ENSUES

[10] And I fell at his feet to worship him. But he said to me, "See that you do not do that! I am your fellow servant, and of your brethren who have the testimony of Jesus. Worship God! For the testimony of Jesus is the spirit of prophecy."

Revelation 19:10

This is the moment when the Ruler of The Universe changes the laws for all time. He declares the testimony of Jesus to be the only legitimate basis for proclamations concerning Heavenly, eternal matters from this moment forth. What is Christ's testimony? All are invited to participate in this New Covenant He has established. The Creator of the universe decrees Universal Law.

The gavel falls.

The Cross has changed everything!

22

Stop The Execution!

De Facto/De Jure

Now what?   Great question. The tyrannical dictator has been defeated. He no longer has the legal authority to rule, reign, govern, dictate, control, demand, execute or imprison. All of his authority has been stripped away.

There was no great 'cosmic battle' between Christ and Satan. Frankly the idea would be laughable were it not so insulting. Jesus Christ, the Word of God made flesh, the One through/with/in/by Whom God created all things. To imagine for a second that Our Lord and King had to stoop to the enemy's level, use the enemy's tactics and had to rise to a place where he could physically dominate and overpower the enemy on a cosmic battlefield puts Jesus and Satan on equal terms. Our Creator has never had to battle to maintain or regain His place in the universe! Ever!

The enemy likes us to think in those terms because it elevates him in our minds and relegates Christ to an imaginary character less than Truth.

Is there a battle? Yes. However, it is not fought on a cosmic battlefield. It is fought inside you.

"Neither shall they say, Lo here! or, lo there! for, behold, the kingdom of God is within you."

Luke 17:21

It stands to reason, if the Kingdom of God is within you, that would also be where the kingdom of darkness operates. I know. I'm not too crazy about it either, but that doesn't make the reality any less true.

The battle between good and evil is currently being fought on seven billion fronts in the lives of every person on this planet. No wonder God has given 'gifts' to help equip us for that battle. To deny the need or reject the gifts is really not such a smart idea. Convincing people to do so is, in fact, a very effective tactic used by the enemy. But that's the subject for another time.[134]

Your weapon is not forged of steel. It is forged of your beliefs. That forces the question that must be answered, "What do I believe?"

The Cross of Christ has given us a legitimate choice. Will I live my life serving God in His Kingdom? Or will I live my life serving Satan in his? How we answer that question determines the way we live our lives.

We are constantly bombarded with 'facts' that blinds us to Truth. Our responsibility is to know Truth and make it fact. What does that mean? That answer is found in legal terms as well: De Jure or De Facto.

When something is 'de jure' it—by law—is legal, and legitimately so. When something is 'de facto' it means something is true by fact, but not officially sanctioned.[135]

Satan had been given the right to rule over men de jure. Humanity simply surrendered their position to him. He ran the global show de jure until the Cross. Christ defeated Satan's kingdom de jure. Fair and square, just and true…Jesus

275

dethroned our enemy in a legal battle in the Courtroom of Creation's God.

This is what Revelation is all about! Satan is defeated de jure; Jesus Christ is the legal King of Kings and Lord of Lords de jure. Humanity has been given the option: serve the ousted ruler by de facto, or serve the crowned ruler by de jure.

[11] "And I saw heaven opened, and behold a white horse; and he that sat upon him was called Faithful and True, and in righteousness he doth judge and make war.

[12] His eyes were as a flame of fire, and on his head were many crowns; and he had a name written, that no man knew, but he himself.

[13] And he was clothed with a vesture dipped in blood: and his name is called The Word of God.

[14] And the armies which were in heaven followed him upon white horses[136], clothed in fine linen, white and clean.

[15] And out of his mouth goeth a sharp sword, that with it he should smite the nations: and he shall rule them with a rod of iron: and he treadeth the winepress of the fierceness and wrath of Almighty God.

[16] And he hath on his vesture and on his thigh a name written, KING OF KINGS, AND LORD OF LORDS."

Revelation 19:11-16

Ancient Jewish court proceedings concerning accusations, convictions and execution of the death penalty involved horses, heralds, and flags. When a person was found guilty and was being led to their execution, at anytime a witness came forward to testify on behalf of the condemned, a flag would be raised—and a horseman raced to the procession, announcing a stay of execution until the new evidence and testimony could be heard.

That's what we are looking at in Revelation 19. Every human being was being led to their execution based on the testimony of their failures, which testified against them. What John has witnessed is the proclamation of humanity's debt of sin being paid in full by Christ Jesus. God has examined the sacrifice and declared it to sufficiently meet the demands of the laws of sin and death. He proclaims man's debt to the law is no longer an issue of the court. Stop the execution!!!!

The horse and rider that blasts out of the courtroom—which John now sees is open—has a message to deliver. "Stop everything!" This can be likened to a Governor granting a stay of execution, or when the leaders of warring countries sign a cease-fire agreement. Laws change at the stroke of a pen. God has ordered a new law govern the lives of humanity. Again

277

John sees a horse and rider dispatched to spread the word by the swiftest means possible in the first century. The rider is The Lord Jesus Christ. The message is man's redemption. The job requires an army.

An army—not in the sense of military might, but in the sheer numbers necessary to complete this mammoth undertaking. The defeated will continue to carry out the previous ruling, "guilty as charged, death to the guilty" de facto.

The masses our King of Kings and Lord of Lords leads are commissioned to carry out the same message. Christ's own garment, dipped in blood is the flag that has been raised to signal the race to stop the execution. That blood was His own that had been mixed with the wine of God's wrath, which Jesus Christ, Himself, endured. The weapons He uses are the Words of Truth declared in Chapter 18.

It would really be wise for the members of His army to know the message they have been commissioned to proclaim. 2 Corinthians 5:11-21 describes it as the ministry, to which we have all been called—the ministry of reconciliation. And John witnessed that 'earth quake'. A shift in earth's power unlike anything experienced before.

The message every person on the planet needs to hear is that the testimony of Jesus is the only legitimate basis for proclamations concerning Heavenly, eternal matters from this moment forth. His testimony: all are invited to participate in this new covenant He has established. The Creator of the Universe has established this eternal, universal law.

Those who join His campaign are given the garments or uniforms reserved for the priests and those who perform the duties of that office.

He Rules with a Rod of Iron.

What does that mean? A rod is either a scepter used by a king to show authority, or it is a staff, used by shepherds to protect and guard. Iron refers to strength.

Jesus Christ rules with authority and strength. Anyone who follows Him with this message is regarded as a priest. The passion and fervor with which He leads this campaign is equal to the passion and fervor with which He suffered the wrath of God.

279

Again, with the sun—

¹⁷"And I saw an angel standing in the sun; and he cried with a loud voice, saying to all the fowls that fly in the midst of heaven, Come and gather yourselves together unto the supper of the great God;

¹⁸ That ye may eat the flesh of kings, and the flesh of captains, and the flesh of mighty men, and the flesh of horses, and of them that sit on them, and the flesh of all men, both free and bond, both small and great.

¹⁹ And I saw the beast, and the kings of the earth, and their armies, gathered together to make war against him that sat on the horse, and against his army.

²⁰ And the beast was taken, and with him the false prophet that wrought miracles before him, with which he deceived them that had received the mark of the beast, and them that worshipped his image. These both were cast alive into a lake of fire burning with brimstone.

²¹ And the remnant were slain with the sword of him that sat upon the horse, which sword proceeded out of his mouth: and all the fowls were filled with their flesh."

Revelation 18:17-21

This is a message to all, but there is a depth of understanding that comes when filtering it through the Covenant of Abraham.

"Therefore leaving the principles of the doctrine of Christ, let us go on unto perfection; not laying again the

foundation of repentance from dead works, and of faith toward God,

² Of the doctrine of baptisms, and of laying on of hands, and of resurrection of the dead, and of eternal judgment.

³ And this will we do, if God permit."

Hebrews 6:1-3

Repent from dead works. That is a foundational principal of the New Covenant. What does it mean? Change your mind concerning the need to perform ceremonial acts to ensure your salvation. Simple as that. What people group had clear instructions from God to physically perform specific rituals for this? The people of Israel.

This sharp sword or truth is that Jesus and his army of ministers literally declares words of truth, "your flesh efforts don't make the grade." Anything you do, in an effort to earn salvation, buy a stay of execution, impress God, and attempt to become righteous is a dead work of the flesh.

All humans do it, but it's going to be especially hard to surrender that way of life when it was specifically mandated by God in the first place. This is why it is important to understand why Jesus assured us that He didn't come to destroy the law, He came to fulfill it—bring to a conclusion, all the aspects necessary to satisfy the requirements of the law of sin and death.

The invitation for the fowls of the air to come and consume the sacrifices made from human effort is to make it very clear that those former covenant ways are no longer necessary, nor will they be accepted in Heaven's Court. Why? Christ's fulfillment make them obsolete.

However, not all acts performed by humans fall in the category of dead works of the flesh. There are things we do, not trying to impress God with our righteousness or earn points on our salvation punch card. Sometimes we do things because we love. Sometimes we do things because we are led by the Spirit of God to do so. Sometimes we do things out of honor, respect, obedience; and sometimes things happen through us because our lives are producing Kingdom of God fruit. The fowls of the air won't be consuming those things. They fall in the category of faith-filled works. It's the fear-filled works that are of no value in God's kingdom and are relegated to bird food.

With this new law firmly established in heaven, legal and binding, the old order of rule is dethroned. Might, fear, death, conquest, control, manipulation, force, elitism, greed and power[137] are no longer the highest laws that govern humanity. Those who insist on lives that march in that army and insist on furthering that style of kingdom will be eternally denied. They will—because of the Cross—never see that type of kingdom exalted over the Kingdom of Heaven. Never.

How is this battle fought? By the truth of God's word.

What if the Cross Changed Everything?

284

23

A Tough Nut To Crack

Have you ever thought it strange how the fall made it possible for sin to capture every human being on the planet, imprisoning them by the letter of the laws of sin and death? Yet the work of Christ in comparison seems so ineffective? That is a problem. A problem, not in actuality, but certainly in our understanding of God's amazing grace and power, which happen to be the major themes of Revelation Chapter 20.

John's vision has shown us the fulfillment of God's plan of man's redemption from the law of sin and death. It has revealed the implementation of the magnificent covenant made between God and Jesus, in which we have been invited to participate. Under the previous covenant, involvement was proven by the physical act of circumcision. This New Covenant is one in which God replaces hard, callous law-of-sin-and-death hearts with hearts of flesh, new hearts, upon which He has inscribed His law.

Circumcision of the heart proves allegiance to this New Covenant. What does that look like? It looks like we stop trying to earn our way into the presence of God by our flesh-motivated attempts at being righteous. Instead, we put all trust in our Lord's righteousness.

In the final chapters of Revelation the readers get a glimpse of the far-reaching effects of the Cross: historically from the fall in the Garden, necessitating the activation of God's plan, presently to its completion and futuristically to its implementation.

Radical Concepts!

Up to this point the references John has used can be found in the Torah, his own eye-witness accounts and Jewish culture, language and symbolism. Beginning in Revelation Chapter 20 John introduces New Covenant language and symbolism. It makes perfect sense for John to do so, as he has just spent 19 chapters reporting on the completion of the previous covenant. This new chapter in human history is such a radical departure from the old that it demands the use of new language, symbolism and imagery. I suspect some of the new was provided by Paul, via his letters to the Churches at Ephesus and Colossae.

Remember when we talked about the literal earthquake, which destroyed three cities in Asia Minor? Well, one of those cities was Colossae. Paul's letter would have circulated throughout the region having the same effect on John's congregation as movies, commercials, books and preachers have on us today. They give common points of reference that direct and influence thought. Take a few minutes and read Colossians and pay particular attention to Paul's description of the church.

Christ is our Head. We are His Body.

Who is the Head of the church[138]? What is the circumcision that proves our devotion to this New Covenant[139]? Where does the body of Christ get its strength and nourishment[140]?

The church is not designed to be a multi-headed monster. Jesus Christ is the head, and we are members of his body. Each one of us has been designed for a specific purpose and function. I cannot tell you what your purpose and function is, but I can tell you what it is not! No other being in the universe is head of His body. That position belongs to Jesus' alone. As members of His body, that means we have lost our heads. I know, icky picture if imagined literally, but it is a symbolic picture of what and how this New Covenant of The Kingdom—a covenant of Grace and Peace—is implemented and realized.

Revelation, Chapter 20 addresses Satan: the limits of his authority, his trial, judgment, sentencing and the execution of that sentence. Satan currently exists in a place of eternal hopelessness, knowing all he desires will never be recognized, honored or implemented.

New Players are Introduced

Christ-followers, whose bodies had already been killed, are given seats of power and authority. They are the judges assigned to hear Satan's case and judge his actions.

This chapter also shows us the heights to which the Lord Jesus Christ has been exalted. His Throne, introduced in verse 11, show us that what had previously been 'business as usual' on earth and in heaven is no longer. Why? Satan has been stripped of any previous authority and ability to enforce the laws that govern sin and death on earth, and he has lost the privilege of having any audience in heaven. The Cross changed everything.

Chapter 20 of Revelation gives us a behind-the-scenes look at this greatest of all 'earthquakes': the coronation of Christ Jesus, Lord of Heaven and Earth and the trial and sentencing of Satan. The court, made up of those souls who had been killed in Satan's campaign to destroy the people chosen to bring Messiah into the world, found him "Guilty as charged."

This amazing chapter also gives us a glimpse at the far-reaching effects of the power of the Cross—the Cross reaching back through time, reinstating the laws of life as introduced when God breathed His life into Adam. It shows us how the Grace of God is able to distinguish and determine deeds motivated by love.

Revelation 20 ends by describing how the court of heaven is able to take the deeds of those who were not privileged heirs to the promises of God, nor were they among the fallen members of the body of Christ. They appear to have been completely unaware of the covenant made between God and Jesus, and were simply were classified as 'the dead.' Those 'dead' are shown in this account to have been given the opportunity to have their deeds judged—which, incidentally, is the way all humanity was to be judged under the law of sin and death. However, something was radically different.

The Cross

Because the only deeds that remain to be tried once everything has passed through the refining process of God's purifying fire are those that had been motivated by love. Everything else, again because of the Cross, is inadmissible in court because that is what it means for the blood of Christ to have purchased our redemption, His sacrifice to be deemed worthy, sufficient and satisfactory!

There is a lot packed into these next 15 verses. This portion of Scripture has been used to condemn humanity by locking them in fear and performance when, in fact, it shows the enemy's eternal demise. I suspect this is the reason behind this chapter having been the single most misinterpreted portion of the entire document. It pertains to the enemy's defeat.

"Wisdom is vindicated by her deeds," Jesus says.

Every dictator knows how powerful fear is. It is the one absolute in a dictator's arsenal. Fear is the result of the fall.[141] Fear is what the Lord commands us not to walk in or be motivated by, and it is the basic tenant of the enemy's kingdom. Revelation Chapter 20 is *the* hinge pin to the fear-fueling, currently popular end-time teachings. So let's see what happens when the hinge swings the other way.

Dispelling fear by searching truth is the motivation for this study. The challenge, at this point does not come from the words on the page. The problem rests in the beliefs of the heart that are products of fear.

Our minds, once they have arrived at a conclusion that satisfies, even if only marginally, can have the most difficult time revisiting anything that it [the mind] has determined to be a settled issue. That concept alone is one of the biggest battles facing new ideas. Thankfully Jesus taught us what to do in His teaching of the wheat and tares parable found in Matthew

13:24-30. The harvest being produced in many hearts, springing from the teachings that have come from Revelation 20 becomes the undeniable indicator that this was a crop of the enemy.

Whenever things such as fear, intimidation, doubt, uncertainty, paralysis, panic and bitterness are the products of a teaching, you need to investigate your heart. Bad seeds produce bad crops. Poor soil produces poor crops. Because Jesus instructs us to pull them up once their fruit is distinguishable, our failure to do so simply propagates the enemy's agenda in our hearts. "Wisdom," Jesus said, "is justified in her children."

24

Thousands, Pits, Thrones & Fires

The opening verses of Revelation Chapter 20 give us what seems to be an unsolvable riddle—a challenge made all the more difficult by previously entrenched concepts, speculative interpretations and accepted teachings. It became necessary to explore the possibility that John used words that had obscure underlying definitions making the message and its meaning for the uninitiated veiled and confusing while—at the same time—remaining obvious to his congregation.

I know we've read this, and the meaning seems so obvious that the idea of revisiting and reinvestigating causes our minds to balk. But let's give our mind permission to consider the possibility that there is something more to be gleaned in this field. Since the literal reading makes no sense and previous attempts to resolve the riddle result in a less-than-satisfying or faith/hope-filled resolution, it is worth the effort to try.

What about "The Thousand Years"?

Apart from the literal translation, what might the phrase, 'a thousand years' mean? When a word is so common-place it becomes very difficult to get our minds to consider obscure meanings or definitions. I think it is wisdom to first rule out the most common definitions and not go off on bunny trails that obscure definitions can lead to. However, if the common, primary definitions lead to dead ends, then it's time to consider the obscure.

I am reminded of the lines from a song that haunted me for years until I applied an obscure definition to a common word, and instantly the song's meaning became crystal clear. The word was 'rent' from the song I'll cover you.

"I think they meant it

When they say you can't buy love

294

Now I know you can rent it."[142]

I was unable to think beyond the obvious definition for rent, which caused my mind to do that mental-contortion thing it does in an effort to make sense of something that is senseless. Then one day rent's more obscure definition rose to the surface: to tear, rip, destroy. Voila, problem solved. The song now makes sense, and I can put that mystery to bed.

The same sort of challenge haunted me with Revelation 20, so I went on a hunt for obscure definitions.

After looking for alternative meanings for the main words: abyss, chain, keys, bound, deceive and coming up empty, I half-heartedly looked at thousand, and this is what I found.

Thousand—what kind of obscure meaning could thousand possibly have? I'm glad you asked!

'Thousand' refers to:

- Family in Judges 6:15
- Tribe of family 1 Sam. 10:19, 23:23
- And towns or cities where families dwell. (Mic. 5:2 speaking of Bethlehem and the cities of Judah)

Yes, they are certainly obscure definitions for any non-Hebrew, but it's doubtful that this portion of John's document tripped them up as it seems to have us.

'Thousand' also conveys the idea of completion and fulfillment.

ARMED WITH THIS INFORMATION, LET'S WADE IN.

A family/tribe/city of dwelling was completed and fulfilled. What does that mean? Lots of speculations are out there, so what's one more worth considering? The first family—fathered by Adam and fulfilled in Jesus (who always referred to himself as the Son of Man)—could be an actual 1,000 years.

Adam lived 930[143] years. Then there is an estimated 3,000 year gap from the time of Adam's fall into the enemy's hands until the birth of Jesus, the seed of woman destined to redeem humanity and crush the authority of the enemy. From Jesus' birth to the destruction of the temple and end of animal sacrifice was 70 years. 930+70=1,000.

Is this a stretch? Perhaps, but keep in mind that Revelation describes the process Christ used in redeeming man from the consequences of Adam's fateful decision. A decision which resulted in the family of man having been loosed from the Life of God and bound to the enemy instead. It is very possible John wanted his readers to be mindful of this.

This option is very appealing by its glaring simplicity. It includes all of humanity. Before Moses, before Abraham, and before Noah, there was Adam. One family defined by a common denominator, redeeming that one family responsible for having brought death to all is also used to bring redemption to all, Jew and Gentile alike.

> *"For if, by the trespass of the one man, death reigned through that one man, how much more will those who receive God's abundant provision of grace and of the gift of righteousness reign in life through the one man, Jesus Christ!"*
>
> Romans 5:17

It is a masterful stroke of genius on par with all the other details overlooked by the enemy.

The other family this might refer to is the family of Abraham. The plausibility of this works well. Remember that one of the conditions that had to be met for redemption to take place was the demand for 12,000 from every tribe, who only ever worshiped God and never strayed from the Covenant of

297

Abraham? It was with those faithful 144,000 Jesus was able to redeem all of humanity.[144]

The 'thousand years' might also be thought of as a criminal sentence imposed by law. This option is also appealing, in that it reinforces the idea of this being a legal proceeding, governed by clear dictates of the law.

And let's not forget the possibility that the 'time of the Gentiles' may refer to the centuries the Nation suffered under foreign rule. As well as the possibility that it could be a combination of options, but, for argument's sake let's do all we can to consider the time to be something in our past as opposed to something in our future. Remember, we've already given the future view plenty of consideration, and have been rewarded with little or nothing for the effort.

[1-3] And I saw a messenger descend from heaven, having the key of the bottomless pit and a powerful bond [one never intended to be released] in his hand.

Satan, the dragon, the devil [accuser, slanderer] the serpent of old was subject to the bond, which contained the power to rule and confine him, and it did so for thousands of years. He is, at this time, relegated to this station, unable to find fulfillment or satisfaction. His incarceration and the seal which is over him ensures no further deception in

unbelief is possible that the time and purpose of the incarceration might be accomplished; after which time it [the bond] must, by necessity, be unbound for his much lesser season.

Revelation 20:1-3 (Author's translation[145])

The bottomless pit. The depths of evil and horror. John first uses this term in Chapter 9 when describing the horror about to be unleashed on the Nation of Judea. The term is used again in Chapter 17 when describing the horrors of the siege and civil war fought in Jerusalem. Now, in Chapter 20, John describes the enemy's arrest and incarceration.

Because of the Cross, things are looking bad for the enemy of our souls.

Christ is exalted, inaugurated, crowned and seated. All authority is given to Him, in heaven and on earth.

Satan has been demoted. He has been disbarred—no longer permitted to enter the presence of God—his arguments are entirely moot. Christ has fulfilled all the requirements necessary for redeeming humanity from the previous governing laws. The new law governing humanity is based in Heaven and Christ's success, rather than on earth and man's failure.

What becomes immediately obvious is that this is talking about the fact that the law of sin and death, to which all creation had become subject, had created limitations for Satan as well. Admittedly, when first seen clearly spelled out, I was taken aback, but I quickly recovered by realizing that of course all creation became limited and subject to the legal confines of the law of sin and death. Satan, out of all the created beings, would certainly be limited, as well. Today, it is the idea that this obvious concept had so eluded me has become the revolutionary one.

These confining limitations, mandated from the Throne, ensured that the enemy would–never see his desire realized. Just as it became necessary for man to be separated from the fruit of life, Satan was separated from something, as well. His sentence wasn't limited to belly crawling, dust eating and heel dodging.

The scope of his arsenal for earth's conquest became limited to what he had already done: deceive humans into believing that they were capable of being god. Granted, that was a pretty far-reaching weapon. It successfully captured every human on the face of the earth (except Jesus), but Satan's resources to escalate beyond that original weapon of deceit, had graciously been cut off. I cannot imagine the destruction that could have ensued had those limitations not been set upon the enemy.

We have examples of criminals, who, although imprisoned, continue to run their kingdom's operation from their prison cells. Thinking in those terms the idea of Satan continuing his conquest, in spite of the legal limitations placed upon him, is not so far-fetched.

We want this verse to mean that the enemy is not able to affect, influence or hinder our lives in anyway. That is simply not the case. His plan, once initiated in the hearts of humanity, continues to produce his desires on this planet.

What these verses also indicate is that there is a limit on the enemy's time of incarceration (although not on the legal limits imposed upon him by that binding seal). Think of this like a prisoner on probation. There are conditions that the convicted is to meet to enjoy a life outside of prison. Failure to comply with the conditions of the probation indicates that the convicted is either unwilling or incapable of living a law-abiding life on their own, and to protect society, those who insist on preying on the innocent are returned to their confined existence. Then, even after the probationary time has expired, there are certain legal confines that remain in place. For example, a person who has a felony conviction is not permitted to have any contact with firearms or ammunition for the rest of their lives. Doing so constitutes another felonious crime, for which they would be charged.

The eternal law imposed upon Satan, binding him to specific confines and limits remained in effect. Even when the Cross of Christ satisfied the requirements for the laws that bound Satan in the first place, that didn't remove the limits in which he was legally authorized to operate. What were those limits? He could use no other tactics to further deceive beyond the one already introduced. Satan was a stickler for the law, and since he insisted on living by the law, he was judged by the law.

This concept gives us much to think about. Let's go back to the garden for a minute. What was the lie used to deceive? 'You can be like God, and establish what is right and what is wrong, what is good and what is evil.' That single lie set humanity on a course of one horror after another.

What happened at the Cross? Well, among other things, mankind was redeemed and no longer under the confines of Satan's rule. By launching a campaign to refute that truth, Satan found himself in violation of the law and was immediately ushered into an existence even more torturous than he had known for 4,000 years prior to the Cross.

Because of his inability to stop the fulfillment of God's iron-clad covenant with Jesus Christ, and the establishment of what constitutes legitimate authority on the earth, Satan's objective is eternally obliterated. Thank you Jesus!

The Cross changed everything! The legal reality that Satan had so skillfully mastered was re-machined and pride blinded him from recognizing his defeat. When he attempted to carry on business as usual, he violated the conditions of his parole. Everything changed because of the Cross, including Satan's job description. Everything had been upgraded to a new operating system making the former obsolete. The new system fixed all the weak areas of the previous by eliminating the problem altogether. He can keep track, keep score, build cases against us for all eternity (which I suspect he will) but the Truth is the Cross supersedes that system.

If you struggle to walk in the reality of all that Christ's Cross implemented, it's because you haven't upgraded to the new operating system. The new programs will not work with the old system.

Let us seriously consider:

The thousand years in Revelation 20: 2 refers to the time between the fall of man in the garden and the redemption of man at the Cross, whether it is a family, city/habitation or sentence fulfilled.

The great chain, is the unbreakable bond established in Heaven's court that kept Satan from succeeding in his plan for absolute control and annihilation of God's creation.

The bottomless pit describes the eternally empty, un-fulfill-able existence that is absent of God, His Life, His Breath, His Purpose, His Love—an apt description of the hopeless existence humans endured under the tyranny of Satan's dictates before Christ redeemed our lives.

Who sat in judgment over Satan's trial?

"And I saw thrones and they sat upon them and judgment was given them the souls of the beheaded be-

304

cause of the testimony (witness) of Jesus and because of the word of God. And whoever worshiped not the beast nor his representative and did not take as their own, the mark upon the forehead nor upon the hand of him and they lived and reigned together in Christ (the anointing) a thousand years."

Revelation 20:4

Thrones to sit upon, and the authority to pronounce judgment is given to those who are members of the body of Christ, of which, Jesus is the Head. Who are they given authority to judge? Satan—an angelic being—created to be a messenger of God and servant to man[146]. Satan, who could never rise above the limits of his created purpose, was a servant to man. Satan, who failed miserably in his mission. And who were the people given authority to hear his case and sit in judgment at his trial[147]? Human beings. The very ones he was created to, but refused to serve. It is easy to imagine Satan demanding to be heard by the Highest court in the universe, but his case is easily decided upon by heaven's newest, most inexperienced residents. Brilliant!

25

Dead are Alive & Living are Dead

When you read other writings attributed to John, you come to recognize his affinity for comparisons of natural things to that of Heavenly, the power of contrast and the irony of paradox. Revelation 20 is a crowning jewel to this testimony.

He reveals that those who are no longer living on the earth are, in fact, alive. Those who lost their heads, ending their physical lives, are very much alive in the presence of God because they chose to make Jesus Christ their head. These same people, destroyed by torture and injustice, whose places are no longer found on earth, have been received and accepted, and they have found their new place in heaven to be of honor and authority as kings and priests.

Whereas, Satan, who had enjoyed a place in heaven as humanity's accuser, discovers his place has been abolished. The accuser becomes the accused. Those he lorded over for four millennia now sit in judgment over him. Oh how the tables have turned. The letter of the law, with which he imprisoned humanity, became the very law which imprisoned him.

Not only are the dead now living, those who insist on remaining bound to the law of death, though they are alive and still breathing air on the earth, are dead. John is bringing his vision, his understanding and his argument home. If, after reading his account of Christ's accomplishments, his friends, colleagues, and the members of his congregation decide to continue their tradition of traveling to Jerusalem, he is power-less to stop them. But, he can be confident that they do so in spite of all the evidence he has provided in an effort to prove that the Old Covenant practice is no longer a necessary re-quirement, in light of Christ's fulfillment of the laws of righteousness.

There has been a changing of the guard, a retroactive implementation of God's original plan and design, a stripping of old laws and an implementation of new. The time to get on board is now, because John knows that Jesus' prophesy concerning the future of Jerusalem is about to be fulfilled.

SATAN'S TRIAL—SHORT AND SWEET

[4]Judgment was given them—the souls of the beheaded because of the testimony of Jesus and because of the word of God- I saw them and the thrones they sat upon.

Whoever worshiped neither the beast nor his representative and did not take as their own the mark upon the forehead nor upon the hand of him, they and Christ lived and reigned together a thousand years.

[5]The remaining [remnant] dead[148] are not alive until it may be completed [brought to a close, paid in full; not to end a thing or state, but to bring about a complete and perfect one].

The thousand years, this one is the preeminent resurrection.

[6]Blessed and holy is the one who has a portion (part) of the preeminent resurrection. The secondary death holds no power in this one.

Instead, priests of God and Christ will they be and they will reign with Him the thousand years.

⁷When the thousand years has been completed it [the bond holding Satan to the confines of God's dictates] will be released.

Satan, out of his prison' ⁸will go forth to deceive the unbelieving in the four corners of the earth-the rulers and their subjects- to join him in the battle against "the number of them as the sand of the sea¹⁴⁹" ⁹and they went upon the breadth of the earth and encircled the camp of the holy and the beloved city [Jerusalem], and fire [in metaphorical expressions: to snatch from danger of destruction] came down from heaven and it devoured them.

(Author's translation) Revelation 20

Type of Fire #1

John seems to be offering hope to his readers by indicating that the lives of those who had been killed or actively being killed during the campaign to destroy the Jewish people, their capital city of Jerusalem, and the Temple, were received and accepted by God. Remember Elijah and the prophets of Baal?¹⁵⁰

"And the devil, the one who deceives, he himself was thrown into the lake of fire and vengeance, joining the beast and the pseudo prophet where they will be examined by words day and night unto the ages forever and ever in that same place."

Revelation 20:10

Type of Fire #2

A lake of vengeance fire. This is definitely not the same fire of acceptance spoken of in verse 9. This indicates something altogether different.

And I saw the earth and heaven flee from the presence of the one who sat on a great (in size and power) white throne. No place was found by them [the beast, pseudo prophet, Satan]. And the dead both great and small, were standing before the throne."

Revelation 20 :11

Who are the dead and what might this mean?

God warned Adam that if he chose to feed off of the Tree of the Knowledge of Good and Evil, death was the sure consequence. Although it took the body nearly a thousand years to cease living, there was a part of man that died immediately when separated from the Source of Life: Adam's soul. Every human being has suffered the same fate; when a human soul is disconnected from God it is dead.

In John's Gospel, Chapter 17:3, we are given Jesus' definition of life: "And this is life eternal, that they might

311

know thee the only true God, and Jesus Christ, whom thou hast sent."

Life is only found in knowing God. And that is only possible because Jesus fulfilled His mission. It is not hard to imagine John's criteria, description and definition for death and life would be the same in both of his writings.

So who are these 'dead?' My guess is everyone, except those who are alive in Christ.

[12] **"Books were opened. And a different kind of book was opened. It is of life. They were separate. The dead had their works written down in the books.**
[13]**The sea**[151] **herself willingly surrendered her dead;**

both death and Hades each surrendered the dead in them. The dead were separated according to their deeds.
[14]**Death and Hades were both thrown into the lake of purifying fire. This is the second death."**

Revelation 20:12-14

Type of Fire #3: Purifying Fire

[15]**And if anyone or anything is not found written in the book of life it is cast into the lake of purifying fire."**

Revelation 20:15

The logical conclusion to be reached concerning a purifying fire is that what has been subjected to purification has been so for a future purpose. If there is no future plan, the exercise is pointless at best, and unimaginably cruel and sadistic at worst. Neither scenario fits with the image of God Jesus came to reveal to us.

Chained, Bound and Bottomless Pit/Abyss

The literal image of these first few verses seem pretty cut and dried. But let's assume there is more to the image than we can see at face value.

When man fell into the plan Satan had proposed, which was simply a no-win situation. That law of sin and death was a bottomless pit, or the abyss, a state of existence that could never be filled, quenched or satisfied. When this law governed humanity, Satan was bound to it as were humans.

This existence is separated and cut off from the life, light and love, which are attributes of God Himself. So, there is absolutely no way life can be lived, light can be seen or love can be experienced in that horrible arrangement man concocted with a little help from Satan.

Just as man was bound to the laws written and ratified on that seven-sealed scroll, so too was Satan bound and sealed by those same laws. The reference to Satan being the serpent of old as well as the mention of deceiving gives a nod to the idea that this is going back to the beginning. Genesis 3:1,13.

And just as a guard was stationed at the garden to keep man from eating of the Tree of Life and losing the chance of redemption altogether, Satan was confined and limited, as well. He could add no other deceptions other than the ones man had already bought into and experienced, which was to be like god, and writing their own version of what will constitute good and what falls in the evil category.

So Satan's arsenal was limited, but he still managed to imprison the whole of humanity in spite of those limitations. Those confines were imposed for a limited time, until that family/tribe /city was completed and fulfilled. Then the bonds be removed though only for a brief time.

This also falls into the idea that John is recording the fulfillment of the law, and everything that changed because of that fulfillment.

That brief season, where Satan was released from the restrictions imposed upon him, saw the horrors of what man is capable of when God is rejected and deceptive lies are given the place that should be occupied by God Himself. The family of man, the tribe of Israel/Judah and the city of Jerusalem all suffered at the fulfillment of the law of sin and death.

Unquenchable, Unrealized Desire Burns Eternally

Then Satan is limited for all eternity when he is cast, alive (still living), in the confines of the lake of fire and brimstone. He will *never* rise above that demoted state. Just as the motives that drove Rome (the beast) and religious pretense (false prophet) would never be a legitimate authority on the earth again, Satan will *never* not burn with the unfulfilled, eternally unrealized desire to rule, reign, control and dictate. Their legitimacy was been unalterably stripped away and eternally replaced by the authority that is Jesus Christ.

There is a new family/tribe/city. God's family, those who are co-heirs with Jesus Christ, the members of His body are the only ones who have been given the legitimate authority and commission to advance the Kingdom of God.

315

26

Full Circle

This has been quite a journey through human history, Biblical history, prophetic history, cultural diversity, legal dealings and repercussions, the fall, Satan, bondage, slavery, sacrifice, Redemption, Covenant, Ascension, and Adoption. An exhaustive study on any one of these subjects could and have filled volumes, but the purpose of this study has been to present options and to encourage exploration and discussion.

Together we have waded through the murky waters known as John's Revelation of all Jesus Christ accomplished. Before we step to the other side of this adventure and walk in the reward He has made available for us to enjoy, let's review some of the areas we have explored:

Reasons for John to have chosen the literary structure and genre used in communicating the message:

- Political climates
- Social climates
- Religious climates
- Cultural climates
- Translation difficulties
- Perspective differences
- Qualifications Jesus had to fulfill to become humanity's Kinsman Redeemer:
  - Passover model
  - Tabernacle/Temple model
  - Annual feast/celebration model
  - Sacrificial offerings model
  - Prophetic model
  - Covenant model
  - Law model
- The Church's responsibilities in the New Covenant described
- Jesus' life and sacrifice on trial:
  - Court/Throne Room
  - Critical players introduced
  - Historical Signatories summoned
  - Symbolism and symbolic language
  - Predetermined, legal criteria presented
  - Ransom required for humanity's freedom from the law of sin and death

- Jerusalem suffers the consequences—warning begins in earnest
  - The horror of Rome's march to Jerusalem (3.5 years)
  - Galilee
  - Valley of Megiddo (Battles of Armageddon)
  - Siege of Jerusalem
- Revealed and explained:
  - The Beast
  - The mark of the Beast
  - 666
  - Multi-horned/headed creature
  - Jesus exalted over all creation
  - Humanity's emancipation declared
  - Satan's trial and sentencing
- Fresh Slate

This brings us full circle. Jesus has succeeded in restoring man's ability to connect and be in relationship with God, our Source of life. The pages of human history have been rolled back, and we are free to live life no longer bound to the laws of sin and death. Today, when we do fail, we are not eternally chained to those failures. To be in Christ means we are not in the enemy.

Like our first ancestors, we also face the Two-Tree choice. However, because of the Cross, our failure doesn't

319

plunge all of humanity into an existence separated from Life. The Cross didn't cause God to become tolerant of sin. No! That idea is ridiculous! Sin continues to destroy our lives, and that is why it is intolerable. Sin must still be paid for with blood from the body of the sinner. It is for this reason the church is legally defined as the body of Christ.

What has changed is that the ransom demands were met. When Jesus ascended to the place of honor and authority and when He took charge, a new and better plan was set in place. Sins are no longer counted[152]—love-motivated deeds are[153].

If a person is kidnapped and held hostage for ransom, when those demands are met and the hostage released, would a sane person continue to pay the ransom and remain captive as though nothing had changed? Absolutely not! Why do we not see the price Christ paid in that same manner? Either the price was paid, once for all, or it was not. If it was not, we are in serious, serious trouble.

Everything has changed! John, after having witnessed the establishment of a new heaven and a new earth, recorded it in Revelation 21. This is another case where—if we insist on a literal interpretation—our minds are forced to concoct any number of suppositions, all of which are relegated to a future fulfillment. This reinforces the idea that what Jesus accomplished was relatively insignificant for the residents of the earth.

On the other hand, if John is using a word-picture to describe the invisible realm of power, authority, spiritual law and the principles that govern the kingdom of Heaven, we have no such need for interpretive speculations. You'll remember that the people who listened to Jesus, while he walked here in the flesh, had a difficult time understanding that he was here to establish Heaven's Kingdom—an unseen realm of righteousness, peace and joy located in the hearts of humanity[154]. Their insistence on the Kingdom of God being physically tangible and operating by the laws that govern the kingdoms of the world made it impossible for them to recognize the reality of what Christ did.

Let's try to not make that same mistake. Going instead with the premise that John is witnessing unseen realms that are real and powerful, nonetheless.

The new heaven John sees is absent of the incessant accuser. I'd say the silence, after 4,000 years of listening to the laundry list of our sins day and night, qualifies as something new. Jesus is now seated on the Throne of all power and authority. New. Those who lived and died during the time between the fall and the Cross have been ransomed and are now in the presence of God. New.

That the new earth is no longer crushed under the tyrannical laws of sin and death is a noteworthy 'new' as well. The only legitimate authority in the earth comes from Jesus Christ. New. The laws by which all creation will be judged are the Laws of Heaven's Kingdom which simply asks, was the action motivated by love? These laws are not carved in stone, they are written by the hand of God on human hearts. New. The Spirit of God is poured out on all flesh. New. Humans are again invited to commune with God, connect with The Source of Life, Love and Wisdom at anytime, anywhere. New. Humanity is no longer a nondescript, mass of sin-held captives lost in anonymity. New. Humans, have been commissioned and empowered to take the message of Christ and how the Cross has changed the dynamics of our earthly existence to every corner of the planet. New.

Other significant things John's testimony tells us is that—unlike the old citadel of Jerusalem built by human effort—this new Jerusalem descends from Heaven. It is a gift from God to the people of the earth and God Himself now dwells among men. It is a magnificent, beautiful gift. This is another glaring disconnect between what many say they believe concerning the presence of God and His accessibility. The interpretations that insist this verse in Revelation has yet to be fulfilled deny His presence in our lives today. Either God is present in our lives right here, right now, or He has to wait for something else to be accomplished before enjoying the type of relationship He had in the beginning, in the Garden, with Adam and Eve.

I believe God's Spirit lives in the hearts of people since the first Pentecost following Christ's Ascension. This belief makes it impossible for me to accept the idea that verse three of Revelation 21 is something yet to be realized. With that as my anchor point, I am forced to look for deeper meanings connected to the promises about death, tears, pain, mourning and crying. They must mean something different than my mind first imagines and my understanding's current limits. Otherwise, the only conclusion I can arrive at is that God lied. Unacceptable. It's time to dig deeper.

Verse four goes on to tell us that all of this is possible because the way things *were* are no longer the way things *are*. What things? How about humanity is no longer imprisoned and suffering under Satan's tyranny for eternity?

Verse five is interesting. The One seated on the Throne commands John to see that He is making all things new. Then goes on to tell him that this reality needs to be recorded because it is true and worthy of trust.

Why? I suggest that although they are easily comprehended in the realm of the Spirit, they are hard to grasp and hold to this side of eternity. Because we are limited in our ability to see beyond our physical confines, having the unseen truths written helps keep us on course. Like on a compass, the written Words of God become our North.

Jesus, as Alpha and Omega, goes on to declare that, "it is done," and already accomplished. You'll remember that this was the name by which Christ revealed Himself to John in the first chapter of Revelation and verse eight. Because this document deals specifically with the Covenant of Redemption, that Christ's Covenant name, Alpha and Omega, speaks to the initiation and fulfillment of God's plan of redemption, rather than His role in the creation completion of the universe.

Again, written documentation and bold declarations reminding us of the Lord's accomplishments will not be necessary when we pass from this life. Those assurances and reminders are needed right now, today.

Our responsibility in this is to remain thirsty for truth. If we do, the reward will be water [truth] from the fountain of Life to slake that thirst. It will also dry tears, heal pain, and end suffering. Because we are, in fact and for all eternity, children of God.

Those who choose to remain faithful to the principles that spring from the enemy (that second tree) will suffer under an existence identical to that prior to the Cross, death. Remember the warning, when you eat of that tree, you will be walking dead. Don't do it! Don't take the bait! Walk in the ways of God, not the ways presented by the world and the enemy of our souls.

The New Teaching of Peace

The word 'jerusalem' means the teaching of peace[155]. It might be a great idea to let the meaning of the word, rather than its geographical namesake, guide our thoughts as we look at what John has to say.

One of the messengers, who participated in the administration of punishment against the sins of the City of Jerusalem, took John to a great, high mountain[156]. This great high mountain[157] is the Government that rests upon Christ's shoulders and is higher than any other government[158].

John goes on to give us a description of this magnificent city of Heaven's habitation on earth. There is no temple because God is no longer limited to the confines of a stone temple. His new tabernacle is in the hearts of humanity.

The foundation stones, each beautiful in their own way, are surprisingly named for the apostles.

The twelve gates forged of pearl are named for the tribes of Israel. It strikes me as odd that the foundation is not built of the tribes of Israel as one might suspect, since they were first. Their part enables access. It is the message of the

New Covenant that provides the foundation. Interesting, isn't it?

The city is perfectly square. This speaks to the fact that this New Jerusalem is possible because of the First Covenant's Faithful of Israel and the New Covenant's Faithful apostles as well. Again we are given the symbol of a measuring rod. Gold represents holiness, purity and heavenly things. This rod measures those qualities, while also telling us that there is adequate room for all! Good news!

The streets are pure, transparent gold. An image we are familiar with, but what might this image represent? I have a theory. Streets are the paths we use to get where we want or need to go. How many times have we found ourselves paralyzed by indecision? Do I go this way or that way? Is this the path God would have me choose, or is it that one? The fear of making the wrong or less-than-perfect choice has arrested their progress, and they do not enjoy the fulfilling life God has made available for His children to walk in. The beauty of this transparent, holy, righteous pavement is that it means you cannot fail. Choose any path, any street, any direction within the boundaries of God's New Jerusalem, His New Teaching of Peace, and that path is going to be a great choice.

Any street, paved in holiness, purity and godly truth is going to lead to life. Stay within the boundaries of His habitation, and you are in a good place. Verses 22-27 describe the beautiful design of this New Teaching of Peace[159].

22 "I saw no temple in the city, for its temple is the Lord God the Almighty and the Lamb. 23 And the city has no need of sun or moon to shine on it, for the glory of God is its light, and its lamp is the Lamb. 24 The nations will walk by its light, and the kings of the earth will bring their glory into it. 25 Its gates will never be shut by day—and there will be no night there. 26 People will bring into it the glory and the honor of the nations. 27 But nothing unclean will enter it, nor anyone who practices abomination or falsehood, but only those who are written in the Lamb's book of life."

Revelation 21:22-27

It is this New Teaching of Peace, The Gospel of Reconciliation, that we have been commissioned as Ambassadors of God's Kingdom, to represent to the nations of the world—nations that have their own identities, their own 'glories.' God embraces the variety, the beauty, the diversity of individuals and cultures. There is room for everyone in the Kingdom, but there is a list of things that are not permitted: whatever is unholy, abominable and untrue.

What has been made and deemed holy?

What is considered abominable in the eyes of God?

What is Truth? And what lies speak against Truth?

These are some great questions. Finding the answers would be time well spent. However, only if you follow the same guidelines employed in this study and recognize that all you think you know and have deemed absolutes will benefit from a closer examination. Remember the guidelines John had to abide when considering how to construct this document? Things that are not permitted in the Kingdom of God include: manipulation, fear, pride, greed, defeat, elitism, accusation, coercion, force, guilt and shame.

Most of us have some serious training to undergo, as we let go of what has been the dictates of our human selves and become proficient with the techniques available to our born-of-God selves. It's a life-long challenge.

27

Paradise Restored

You Are What You Eat

The final chapter in Revelation shows another comparison. That of the Garden described in Genesis (before the fall) and the Beauty of God's plan restored.

Jesus' Teachings 101: Parable of the Sower[160]. The Lord told us that we had to understand this Kingdom parable because it was the key to understanding all the parables. Then He broke it down for us:

[11] "Now the parable is this: The seed is the word of God. [12] The ones on the path are those who have heard; then the devil comes and takes away the word from their hearts, so

that they may not believe and be saved. [13] *The ones on the rock are those who, when they hear the word, receive it with joy. But these have no root; they believe only for a while and in a time of testing fall away.* [14] *As for what fell among the thorns, these are the ones who hear; but as they go on their way, they are choked by the cares and riches and pleasures of life, and their fruit does not mature.* [15] *But as for that in the good soil, these are the ones who, when they hear the word, hold it fast in an honest and good heart, and bear fruit with patient endurance."*

Luke 8:11-15

The Word of God is the seed. Human hearts are the gardens where those seeds grow. The quality of those hearts determine the quantity of the yield.

Using the Lord's first parable, let's revisit Genesis 2:6-14.

God established a garden where Eden (pleasure) originates. It is in that place God put the man, who had become a living soul by the very Breath of God. Every kind of tree [(source) philosophy, science, school-of-thought, ministry, purpose] was found in that garden, including the source for life [Knowledge of God] and the source which leads to death [the dichotomous belief of good and evil]. A river flows through the garden, to water it and help bring to life the trees planted there.[161] That river, after flowing through the garden, comes out on the other side and splits into four separate and distinct branches[162]:

The most prominent of the four distributaries is Pishon which means increase,[163] and that increase is in connection with gold and riches.

The second of the four distributaries is Gihon, which means to burst forth and it surrounds the land of Ethiopia (black).

The third is Hiddekel, meaning rapid, which flows toward the East (the start and beginning) of Assyria ,which means success and advancement.

The fourth is Euphrates, which means fruitfulness.

What Could this Mean?

I think it means that God Himself supplies us with the water that brings life to our hearts. When that fountain of life leaves the limits and boundaries of our inner-man, it supplies life to earthly pursuits as well:

- Enterprise, wealth, provision, artistry (gold, precious stones)
- Unknown, unseen, unexplored (black)
- Advancement in technology, science and understanding (rapid advance)
- Family life (fruitfulness)

God's truths flow through human hearts, causing desires to grow. Those desires are pursued during our lives on earth.

When man rejected God as the motivating source for life and living, accepting instead the dichotomous philosophy of good and evil, everything became perverted, twisted and unrighteous.

With God's Truth cut off from our life pursuits, no life, pleasure, satisfaction or fulfillment could ever be realized. Amassing riches became the primary means by which humans attempt to find fulfillment, identity and purpose. Searching the unknown reaches of wisdom and understanding devolved into a fascination with demonic doctrines, occult practices, and wicked pursuits. Advancement in science, discovery and knowledge turned into war, murder and conquest. And the design for family so deteriorated that spouses and children are often seen only for the labor they can perform or the inconvenience they bring.

Death settled over, contaminated and destroyed everything. Worst of all, there was no way to reinstate the Life of God. The way back to God's Delightful Garden was blocked. The ability to find pleasure in our heart-desires, nurtured by the Life of God, was gone. What a sad, miserable existence man had plunged into. This is why God moved heaven and earth to redeem His beloved creation.

Now, let's look at what John has to say about the living conditions of those who accept what Jesus did for them.

Revelation 22

There is a river. Unlike the river described in Genesis, which started as one and divided into four; this river begins as two tributaries and becomes one. Tributary one originates from the Throne of God, Ruler and Creator of the universe. Tributary two flows from the Sacrificed Lord, Jesus Christ.

This river flows through the middle of the street of the new teaching of peace. Just like the streets, the river is also transparent. This life-giving water of truth is crystal clear.

335

There are not two trees in this image, only one. But this massive tree is on either side of the magnificent, life-giving river of Truth. The fruits it produces is capable of feeding every human need. The leaves of this life-sustaining source heals the nations. Those nations that we learned in the previous chapter where welcomed into the New Jerusalem, they were to bring their unique glories, personalities, strengths, and identities. Anything from that list that needs to be adjusted and healed, will find that healing in the leaves of the tree of life. How? I have no idea, but I cannot wait to see it in action.

Curses, they no longer play any role in this new teaching of peace. God's Authority and the testimony of The Lamb have the final say in this place. His servants, He has marked them as His very own. They are able to look upon His face and worship Him, no longer veiled in darkness, but in the full light of His Glory. This is an eternal arrangement.

The messenger, that same angel, told John that these things are all trustworthy and true. And because the Lord God has now revealed this to his servants, it indicates that what he has witnessed must soon take place[164].

Look! Pay attention! I am coming soon! Who is coming soon? The same angel who has been John's tour guide since Rev. 21:9; identified as being one of the angels commissioned to carry out the vengeance, which is about to be unleashed on the earthly City of Jerusalem. It is for this reason that anyone who pays attention to the words of this Revelation is going to be blessed (happy and empowered)! Because they won't be showing up and hanging out in Jerusalem anytime between now and when this messenger is released to carry out the sentencing against that city.

John is overwhelmed with what he has witnessed. So much so that he falls in worship at the feet of this angel. He gets reprimanded for it, taught and corrected, but thanks be to God he didn't get decommissioned! Instead, he is ordered to write everything revealed. He is instructed to not seal the word he writes because there is no time.

Verse 11 seems to be a bit harsh when it is first read, but all it means is there is no time left.[165] John's overwhelming desire to pastor people makes him take time, put forth effort and do whatever is necessary to help people. The angel is telling him that getting this message out is now John's number-one priority.

When I am faced with a major task with dire consequences for failure, I have to remind myself that there are some things that only I can do, and I need to focus on doing those things. There are things that need to be done, but others are able, and when I don't have the time to do everything, even if I might want to, I have to trust that others will see those things through. This is especially difficult when it comes to Godly, noble, Kingdom of Heaven sorts of things.

Jesus joins the conversation. He assures John that He, Himself, will address those issues that threaten to sidetrack his commission to get this warning out. "I am the Alpha and the Omega, the First and the Last, the Beginning and the End. I am coming soon, and my reward is with me. I will repay according to everyone's work."

Those who wash their robes, are to be granted the right to eat, once again, from the tree of life and enter into this new teaching of peace are blessed! There are things not permitted on the premises of God's Holy Habitation, this New Teaching of Peace. They include the wicked practices of the enemy's kingdom: sorcery, fornication, murder, idol worship and those who love and practice falsehood.

Jesus reminds John that He sent the angelic messenger with this testimony to him in the first place, as the One Who fulfills the promise made to David (that his descendants would sit on the Throne forever).

The invitation goes out to all who are thirsty and wish to take God's offered gift of life-giving water. Who does the inviting? God's Spirit, the Bride and everyone who comprehends this message. They all have one thing to say, "Come."[166]

In verses 18-19 John ties up some legal loose ends. It's like a wedding officiate asking if there is anyone who has just cause that these two should not be wed. It's a legal formality, though it rarely results in a halted ceremony, it is still necessary.

All covenants when declared, have both blessings and curses attached to them. The purpose is to give the parties of the covenant reminders of just how binding and far-reaching their agreement is to be.

Jesus signs off on the testimony and agrees to what is written. "Surely I am coming soon," He says.

John finishes the legal document by agreeing with and notarizing that it is, indeed Jesus Christ, who is The One promising to come soon, Amen (so be it).

John adds a postscript, which is a prayer of declaration and a reminder to his readers to access the power and ability that is available to them. The word grace means God's power and ability working through us to accomplish His will.

The grace of the Lord Jesus be with all the saints. Amen.

We have a huge task ahead of us. We have been entrusted with the ministry of reconciling people back to God. Simply put, Jesus Christ rules and reigns. He loves people. All people! And He is waiting with open arms to welcome them home.

Thank you Lord Jesus! You Changed Everything!

Notes

Introduction

[1] To hear what others are saying about the doctrine of dispensations, I suggest viewing The Late Great Planet Church, The Rise of Dispensationalism. DVD available at www.americanvision.org

Chapter 1 Purpose~Meaning~Relevance

[2] In fact the "good stuff" is all for us. And there is a lot more 'good stuff' than the last couple of chapters. We just need to know what we are looking for.

[3] Luke 19:41-44, Luke 21:20-22.

[4] Matthew 24:1-2, Mark 13:1-2, Luke 21:5-7

[5] Luke 21:32

[6] Matthew 20:25-28

[7] Luke 21:32

[8] The forty-year transition period is reinforced throughout Jewish history. Most notably the time Moses spent after fleeing Egypt before returning to deliver the people from bondage. Then there was the forty years spend in the wilderness to raise and train a generation capable of reclaiming the Promised Land. Transition takes time.

[9] Laodicea was one of three cities completely destroyed by earthquake(s) between 60-62AD. It was also the only city of the tree to rebuild; Colossae and Hieropolis did not.

[10] Written in early 300AD, covering Church history from Christ to 324AD.

[11] Luke 10:26

Chapter Two Someone Else's Mail

[12] Ancient Hebrew Lexicon of the Bible, Benner, Jeff.

[13] Through the centuries many have argued the superior value of one translation over another. Every translation is made through the paradigm of the one doing the translating. It is far more important that the translator be in a love relationship with the Lord, have a heart that Is whole and embraces His Love. This makes it possible for the Spirit of God to be more easily communicated. It is no great mystery that translations commissioned for political gain, power and control somehow retain that flavor.

341

The higher argument must be, "do I know Him?" No translation is an adequate substitute for being in an honest, fulfilling relationship with the One of Whom the Scriptures speak.

[14] John 14:26, I John 2:27

[15] There is overwhelming evidence, both historical and linguistic, indicating the New Testament texts were originally written in Hebrew. Recent archaeological discoveries have found that Hebrew was not a "dead language" (as was previously thought). A quick online search will produce enough websites provide information that leads to the conclusion that the original New Testament texts were written in Hebrew. www.yashanet.com is one such site.

[16] *The Ancient Hebrew Lexicon of the Bible, Hebrew Letters, Words and Roots Defined Within Their ancient Cultural Context* by Jeff A. Benner.

[17] *Old Testament Reference in the Book of Revelation.* Dr. Arnold G. Fruchtenbaum, ThM., PhD.

Chapter Three More Than A Greeting

[18] 'Messenger' and 'angel' are translations of the same Greek word.

Chapter Four Legal Documents

[19] www.greattreasures.org

[20] The 2011 edition of the South Carolina Court Reporter Manual pages 32 and 33 states:

A statement must be made by the court reporter certifying the accuracy of the transcript. The certificate must be signed by the reporter.

A court reporter's signature on any required report constitutes a certificate by him/her that the information entered …is true and accurate to the best of the court reporter's knowledge. (Bold emphasis is as it appears in manual.)

[21] There was only a brief time in history where seven churches existed in Asia Minor.

[22] An island located 63 miles south/West of John's home in Ephesus. "Finds from various excavations show that the island was inhabited in the 5 century BC." www.destinationgreece.com

[23] James 1:2-8

[24] www.religiouslyincorrect.com/Articles/TriCityAreaEarthquake.shtml

[25] www.sacred-texts.com/cla/tac/a14020.htm

[26] Robinson, J. 1976. *Re-dating the New Testament*. The Westminster Press, Philadelphia, PA. pgs. 197-228, 316-317.

[27] Robinson, J. 1976. Re-dating the New Testament. The Westminster Press, Philadelphia, PA. p14.

Chapter Five A Coded Message

[28] The word 'apocalypse' is the transliteration of the Greek word which means 'revelation'.

[29] Apocalyptic Literature was first introduced to the Jewish audience during the time of their captivity in Babylon by Daniel and Ezekiel. http://www.jewishencyclopedia.com/articles/1643-apocalyptic-literature-neo-hebraic
There are many sources that give insight into the art of interpreting Apocalyptic Literature.

[30] This is similar to works by C.S. Lewis and J. R. R. Tolkien, The Chronicles of Narnia, and the Lord of the Ring respectively. Both of which were also written during a time of war, then the authors' nation was being overrun and conquered.

[31] The Day of the Lord does not mean Sunday or Saturday. The Day of the Lord refers to judgment of some sort. The Day of the Lord, The Day of Judgment, The Day of Atonement are all references to the Jewish Feast Day: Yom Kippur. http://jewishroots.net/holidays/day-of-atonement/yom-kippur.htm

[32] Falls in March and/or April of the Gregorian Calendar

[33] Falls in September and/or October of the Gregorian Calendar

[34] Leviticus 23:23-25, Numbers 29:1-6, Psalm 81:3-4, Ezra 3:1-6, Nehemiah 8:1-12

[35] Read Nehemiah 8:1-18 to see what happened the first celebration of the feast by those returning to Jerusalem after having spent 70 years in captivity.

[36] Yom Kippur/The Day of Atonement/The Day of Judgment is exactly four months (to the day) after Pentecost. – Yeah, it matters.

[37] Land of approximately 300 square miles, or roughly the size of Dallas/Fort Worth, TX.

[38] James 2:13

Chapter Six The Ultimate Sacrifice

[39] The Tabernacle was the mobile tent structure built during the time Moses was leading the people. It was built by the specifications given to the Israelites by God, Himself.

[40] A cubit is roughly 18 inches. This gate was 30' wide.

[41] Jesus said, "I am the gate" John 10:9.

[42] Leviticus Chapter 16

[43] Hebrews 2:17 & 18, Hebrews 4:14 & 15

[44] Exodus 34:29-35

[45] Winston Churchill describing WWII-era Russia.

Chapter Seven Covenants

[46] This is very similar to the description we have of the Lord's presence during the 40 years the Israelites were in the wilderness: a pillar of cloud during the day, a pillar of fire during the night. Exodus 13:21

[47] Genesis 3

Chapter Nine Doors, Thrones, Scrolls & Seals

[48] The letters to the churches are listed in their geographical order. There had been nine churches, but a major earthquake between 60 and 62 AD destroyed the cities of Hierapolis, Colossi and Laodicea. Laodicea is the only one of the three to rebuild, bringing total number of churches in this region to seven.

[49] Genesis 3:24

[50] Genesis 2:8-3:13

[51] The word "Eden" means pleasure and delight.

[52] Read Galatians Chapter 5 and Ephesians Chapter 5 for a list of life-sustaining fruit we are capable of producing while we walk on this earth.

[53] 'With a rod of iron' does *not* mean bludgeon and punish. A rod is a scepter of authority like a king would use or a staff of protection and defense like a shepherd would use.

[54] A first-century Jewish marriage consisted of the promise of betrothal, then the groom would spend the next several months to a year preparing a place (usually a room in his father's house). When his father was satisfied with the son's efforts he (the father) would give the go ahead for his son to

go and get his bride. This usually took place in the night and was referred to as "a thief in the night."

Chapter Ten Witnesses Summoned

[55] 'Ginomai' is in the aorist tense which usually means the action took place in the past. In which case - the last phrase could easily say 'which came with or as a result of this.

[56] To loosen what is fast bound; hence, to unbind; greattreasures.org.

[57] A beautiful account of this practice is described in the Book of Ruth.

[58]

http://penelope.uchicago.edu/Thayer/E/Roman/Texts/secondary/SMIGRA*/Testamentum.html

[59] http://www.trismegistos.org/seals/overview_3b.html

Chapter Eleven Emancipation!

[60] Four spirits of the heavens - Zechariah 6:1-8 - are also described as horses.

[61] The Living Creature is commanding the rider (witness) to appear in court to watch the seal- breaking / document-opening ceremony.

[62] Adam's other actions and responses in this situation also set the course for what is known as the doctrine of predestination. In verse 12, Adam infers that none of this would have happened had God not brought Eve into the mix in the first place. The suggestion being that this was ultimately God's fault. The appetite for irresponsibility is a direct result of the fall.

[63] These four also correspond to the first four letters of the Hebrew alphabet http://www.ancient-hebrew.org. One = Leader, Two = Family, Three = Gather, Four = Door. What does that mean? When the leader changed, the family of humanity changed. The earth's ability to freely yield nourishing crops changed, and the door is now wide open to death, disease, pestilence and conflict.

[64] Romans 10:4

[65] Leviticus 17:11 "For the life of the flesh *is* in the blood, and I have given it to you upon the altar to make atonement for your souls; for it *is* the blood *that* makes atonement for the soul."

[66] We use the same terminology today when we say we operate under the laws which govern our actions, be they Federal, State or local. Those laws are over us, and we operate under them.

[67] Col. 2:17 author's translation

[68] http://greattreasures.org

[69] Romans 8:19-22 [19] For the earnest expectation of the creature waiteth for the manifestation of the sons of God. [20] For the creature was made subject to vanity, not willingly, but by reason of him who hath subjected the same in hope, [21] Because the creature itself also shall be delivered from the bondage of corruption into the glorious liberty of the children of God. [22] For we know that the whole creation groaneth and travaileth in pain together until now.

[70] A portion of the Song of Moses gives us a hint Deut. 32:7-9 [7] Remember the days of old, consider the years of many generations: ask thy father, and he will shew thee; thy elders, and they will tell thee. [8] When the Most High divided to the nations their inheritance, when he separated the sons of Adam, he set the bounds of the people according to the number of the children of Israel. [9] For the LORD's portion is his people; Jacob is the lot of his inheritance.

[71] http://www.ancient-hebrew.org/28_chart.html

[72] Matthew 27:50-54
http://www.biblicalarchaeology.org/daily/biblical-topics/crucifixion/jesus%E2%80%99-crucifixion-reflected-in-soil-deposition/Geological sediment indicate a localized earthquake occurred sometime between 26 AD and 36 AD.

[73] Matthew 28:18; Colossians 2:13-15

[74] Matthew 27, Mark 15, Luke 23

[75] Joseph, was one of Jacob's sons and a great-grandson of Abraham. You will remember Jacob was the man whose name was changed to 'Israel' and who fathered 12 sons. Those sons became the nation of Israel.

[76] http://www.ancient-hebrew.org/56_home.html

[77] http://www.blueletterbible.org/study/larkin/dt/29.cfm

[78] http://www.ancient-hebrew.org/56_home.html

Chapter Twelve John's Warning Begins
[79] John 1:29

[80] A person marked on their forehead, in first century Rome, was a slave. Symbolically speaking when God instructed the people of Israel to write the Word of God on their foreheads and bind them on their hands: Deuteronomy 6:5-9, He was instructing them to let His Word guide their thoughts and actions.

[81] Matthew 27:50-54

Chapter Thirteen Groundwork Is Laid

[82] Ezekiel 16, Hosea, Jeremiah 3. In all of these references God offers to maintain the covenant if the nation would return to Him. The choice to return was theirs to make. He does not use force.

[83] Matthew 24:34, John 19: 37, Zechariah 12:10-14

[84] *Repent* simply means a change of heart and mind.

[85] For those who were unable to participate in Passover because of illness or being ceremonially unclean from having handled a dead body, God made provision. A second Passover was held one month after the first. Numbers 9:1-12.

[86] *The Complete Works of Flavius-Josephus*, William Whiston translation, 1901 Thompson & Thomas, public domain.
Roman Historian, Cornelius Tacitus also makes reference to these events in *Histories, Book V.*

[87] Josephus' *Antiquities of the Jews* book 20, chapters 8 - 11 would be a good starting point.

Chapter Fourteen Jerusalem Implodes

[88] Matthew 24, Mark 13, Luke 21.

[89] http://jewishroots.net/library/miscellaneous/high_priest_corruption.html

[90] http://jewishroots.net/library/miscellaneous/high_priest_corruption.html

[91] There are three accounts concerning this event: Josephus' writing in *Antiquities of the Jews*, Hegessipus as quoted by Eusebius, and Clement of Alexandria. They differ in specifics, but share the general message James suffered a brutal death because he refused to renounce his trust in Jesus Christ as Lord and Savior.

[92] Josephus reports that no fewer than 3 million men assembled for Passover in 65AD made appeal to Cestius to alleviate their misery by reining in this tyrant. Their pleas fell on deaf ears.

[93] "The whole administration of Florus is marked by the same cruelty and oppression—the same reckless and merciless tyranny: while the conduct of the Jews is not unstained by treachery to the Romans, particularly in their slaughter of the Roman guards in the castle of Antonia, after having laid down their arms on terms of peace. This latter insult brought up Cestius from Syria, with an immense army, who besieged Jerusalem; and certainly had he continued the siege at that time, the Jews had sooner met the fate which hung over them; but by one of the unaccountable circumstances which, however mysterious to the mere worldly mind, marks so strongly the interposition of Divine Providence, Cestius raised the siege and fled from Jerusalem, pursued and discomfited by the Jews; and having thus tarnished the glory of the Roman arms, prepared for the unhappy Jews, all the horrors which awaited them, during the war carried on by Vespasian.

On this occasion, however, through the mercy of God, the Christians in Jerusalem found the means of their preservation; for the great tribulation which was brought upon the nation by the conduct of Cestius, in besieging the city, led those who remembered the words of the Lord, "when ye shall see the abomination of desolation," (or the Roman ensigns, on which were the idolatrous images of the heathen,) spoken of by Daniel the prophet, "stand in the holy place, then let them which be in Judea flee into the mountains. For there shall be great tribulation, such as was not from the beginning of the world, no, nor ever shall be." The Christians in Jerusalem, recalling this prediction, made their escape, upon the retreat of Cestius, out of the city, and fled to Pella beyond Jordan, and to the mountains of Perea. Or to use the words of Josephus, - though he knew not the cause of their flight,- "After this calamity which had befallen Cestius, many of the most eminent Jews swam away from the city, as from a ship that was going to sink." *The Destruction of Jerusalem*, Pierre, 1827.

[94] Eliezer Posner, The Meaning of Three, chabad.org.

[95] Isaiah 37:27

[96] John chapter 4

Chapter Fifteen No More Delay

[97] Matthew 24:21

[98] Josephus *Jewish Wars* 5.1.4

[99] Tacitus *Histories 5.12;* see also Josephus *Jewish War 5.6.248–57*

[100] The details and horror of these 5 months are recorded by Josephus in Jewish Wars. As well as the Roman Historian Tacitus' accounts. http://www.josephus.org/FlJosephus2/warChronology7Fall.html offers an easy-to-understand overview and timeline of the Fall.

[101] Luke 21:20-24

[102] "For these be the days of vengeance, that all things which are written may be fulfilled." Jesus Christ when speaking of the time that the temple in Jerusalem would be completely destroyed, Luke 21:22

[103] http://www.caerleon.net/history/army/page5.html
Signifer Corniculario with various signs and Roman (from the Trajan column), Giovanni Battista Piranesi, public domain.

[104] A statement that would have been grounds for death, had John not been communicating in this coded manner.

[105] Ruin, destruction

[106] Destroyer

[107] Genesis 15:18-21

[108] Things were bad enough. Israel, by this time, had already splintered into two nations: Israel and Judah. Ten of the tribes formed the nation of Israel, and two became Judah. Israel had been conquered during the Assyrian conflict and dispersed, within a few generations their heritage and connection to their ancestors was lost in the sea of humanity. Judah, the remnant, maintained their nation's heritage and continued the sacrificial system of atonement for sin—the system Christ came to fulfill. It was absolutely imperative for all of mankind that this tiny nation remain until Christ could come. These four angels had been commissioned with the task of keeping the lines of separation clear.

Chapter Sixteen It's Pivotal

[109] The Eastern mind tends to thinks this *and* that. The Western mind tends to think this *or* that.

[110] Zechariah describes a very similar vision in his book of prophesy, Chapter 4. The difference between John's vision and Zechariah's is the Old Covenant vision had one candlestick; John's New Covenant vision has two.

Chapter Seventeen Politics Is A Beast

[111] http://www.conservapedia.com/Chiasmus

[112] http://village.hcc-nd.edu/hodonnell/JohnBTB.htm

Chapter Eighteen Harvest Celebrations
[113] Daniel also prophesied very clearly concerning the Messiah.
[114] Genesis 32:12
[115] *Nero fastened the guilt and inflicted the most exquisite tortures on a class hated for their abominations, called Christians* [or Chrestians] *by the populace"* (Tacit. *Annals* XV)
[116] http://www.randomhistory.com/2008/07/26_tattoo.html
[117] www.vanishingtattoo.com/tattoo_museum/greek_roman_tattoos.html

Chapter Nineteen Croaks & Plagues
[118] http://www.bje.org.au/learning/judaism/holydays/festivals/pilgrim.html
[119] An indelible mark made on the soldier's hand with a hot iron or tattoo.
[120] John 4:34-35
[121] http://www.mountainretreatorg.net/bible/numbers.html

Chapter Twenty Brides, Beasts, Horns & Harlots
[122] Genesis 3:15
[123] http://www.ligonier.org/learn/devotionals/covenant-curses/
[124] The only times frogs are mentioned in the bible are in connection with the events in Egypt at the time of Israel's deliverance.
[125] Jesus accomplished the first half of this whole, the 3 ½ years from the time of His baptism through the crucifixion.
[126] Cline, E. H., (2000) *The Battles of Armageddon: Megiddo and the Jezreel Valley from the Bronze Age to the Nuclear Age.* Ann Arbor, Michigan: University of Michigan Press.
[127] Josephus, *Jewish Wars* 3.4.1 63
[128] http://www.josephus.org/FlJosephus2/warChronology5Pg3.htm
[129] Describing 1st century Jewish marriage customs: http://www.foundationsmin.org/studies/bridegroom.htm
[130] The city of Megiddo "is widely regarded as one of the most important sites in the entire Near East. As the current excavators of the site have described…From its advantageous location, Megiddo controlled one of the most important roads in the ancient world, the Via Maris. This was an international military and trade route that ran between Egypt in the south

and Syria, Phoenicia, Anatolia, and Mesopotamia in the north and east…Megiddo had great strategic significance, for whoever controlled the city and maintained an army there would dominate this vital international route." Cline, E. H. (2000) The *Battles of Armageddon: Megiddo and the Jezreel valley from the bronze age to the nuclear age*. Ann Arbor, Michigan: University of Michigan Press.

[131] www.blueletterbible.org

[132] Pride is the absence of humility. To be humble is to trust God's ways, words and perspective more than we do our own.

Chapter Twenty-One Stop The Execution!

[133] Abraham had promised his posterity in covenant to The One True Living God. The Nation of Israel is God's betrothed.

Chapter Twenty-Two A Tough Nut To Crack

[134] Satan Unmasked, by Dr. James B. Richards is an excellent resource on this subject.

[135] http://onlinelaw.wustl.edu/legal-english-de-factode-jure/

[136] http://www.jewishvirtuallibrary.org/jsource/Talmud/sanhedrin6.html

[137] Which are all of the principles that Rome and any other ungodly authority use to build their kingdoms.

Chapter Twenty-Three Thousands, Pits, Thrones & Fires

[138] Col. 1:18-24

[139] Col. 2:11-18

[140] Col. 2:19-3:15

[141] Genesis 3:10 When God asked Adam why he was hiding, "I was afraid," was Adam's reply.

Chapter Twenty-Four Dead Are Alive & Living Are Dead

[142] Finster & Lucy Music Ltd. Co., Universal Music Corp. Lyrics by Jonathan D. Larson

[143] Information as readily known to the first century readers as it is to us because it's found in Genesis 5:5 of the Pentateuch.

[144] Revelation Chapter 7

[145] By using www.greattreasures.org

[146] For an in depth study of this subject, I highly recommend Satan Unmasked by Dr. James B. Richards

[147] 1 Cor. 6:3

Chapter Twenty-Five The New Teaching Of Peace

[148] The word 'dead' is an adjective, it is not a noun or verb, it is a word used to describe or indicate a particular noun: The Remaining or Remnant.

[149] Remember, this figure of speech was used by God when He described his promise to Abraham concerning his descendants.

[150] Read 1 Kings 18, verses 30-39 in particular.

[151] Sea: humanity Isaiah 60:5

Chapter Twenty-Six Full Circle

[152] 2 Corinthians 5:18-21

[153] Revelation 20:12&13

[154] Luke 17:21

[155] www.blueletterbible.org

[156] You will remember that mountains are a symbolic representation of governing authorities.

[157] Micah 4:1

[158] Isaiah 9:1-7

[159] Peace as defined by Christ: because of the Cross, there is now peace between God and man.
For more on this subject: The Gospel of Peace, by Dr. James B. Richards.

Chapter Twenty-Seven Paradise Restored

[160] Found in Matthew 13, Mark 4 and Luke 8.

[161] This is different from the mist that was the water source described for the rest of the earth.

[162] Earth science tells us that this is opposite of the natural progression of a river, where the small branches (tributaries) flow into and feed the larger river. Rarely does a large river disperse and divide into smaller.
http://geography.about.com/od/waterandice/a/Bifurcation-Of-Rivers.htm

[163] www.blueletterbible.org

[164] This verse is the second time in the Revelation where we are told that at the time of its writing, what had been revealed that had yet to be accom-

plished would occur soon. 66 AD would definitely qualify if John was writing this in 64 or 65 between the Great Fire of Rome and Nero's suicide.
[165] Another testimony to the fact that, at its writing, there was not thousands of years to see its fulfillment. Although, it's sad to realize that because people have been taught to believe that these warnings are for the 21st century church that this attitude in particular has been adopted; 'There is no time left to share the gospel with those who might require more than a tract and a 30 second prayer'.
[166] 2 Corinthians 5:11-19

What if the Cross Changed Everything?

www.ingramcontent.com/pod-product-compliance
Lightning Source LLC
LaVergne TN
LVHW051620080426
835511LV00016B/2092